ZOJIRUSHI RICE COOKER COOKBOOK

Easy, Delicious, and Always Perfect Cooking for Everyday with Zojirushi Rice Cooker

Annabelle Foster

Copyright

TABLE OF CONTENTS

Introduction

● ● ●

Zojirushi Rice Cooker Cookbook" by Annabelle Foster is the best way to learn how to use the Zojirushi Rice Cooker to make cooking easy, tasty, and always perfect.

This whole cookbook will take you on a journey through food that will change the way you make everyday meals. There is no need to be a good cook to have the Zojirushi Rice Cooker. It will make cooking easier and better for everyone.

There are a lot of different kinds of recipes in this cookbook, from hearty breakfasts to delicious desserts, so there is something for everyone and every occasion. Get creative with rice and make new, tasty dishes. Also, find tasty side dishes that go well with any meal and tempting main dishes that you'll want to make again and again.

However, the Zojirushi Rice Cooker can do more than cook rice. It's a flexible kitchen appliance that can make a lot of different foods. Soups and stews will warm you up, flavors from around the world will awaken your taste buds, and desserts will make you say "yes" to your sweet tooth.

This cookbook's recipes are written clearly and precisely, and each one comes with clear instructions, helpful hints, and beautiful pictures to help you along the way. With the Zojirushi Rice Cooker Cookbook, every meal will be a culinary success, whether you're cooking for yourself, your family, or guests.

Come on this cooking adventure with Annabelle Foster and find out what your Zojirushi Rice Cooker can really do. The Zojirushi Rice Cooker makes cooking easy, delicious, and always perfect. Say goodbye to stress in the kitchen and hello to meals that are works of art.

What is Rice Cooker Cookbook?

● ● ●

A Rice Cooker Cookbook is a collection of recipes that are made to be cooked in a rice cooker. Most of the time, these cookbooks have a lot of different recipes, from simple meals made with rice to more complicated ones that use the rice cooker's many functions to cook different grains, proteins, vegetables, and even desserts.

A Rice Cooker Cookbook has step-by-step instructions that are specific to how to use a rice cooker, as well as helpful hints for getting the best flavor and texture. These cookbooks are often written for a wide range of people, from new cooks looking for quick and easy meal ideas to seasoned chefs looking for new ideas for dishes they've never made before.

Some things that all Rice Cooker Cookbooks have in common are:

Foods like rice, grains, soups, stews, and more, and groups of recipes for breakfast, lunch, dinner, and dessert are included.

Help with choosing the right type of rice cooker and understanding how it works.

How to change traditional recipes so that they can be cooked in a rice cooker.

Unique and creative recipes that make the most of what the rice cooker can do.

In general, a Rice Cooker Cookbook is helpful for anyone who wants to get the most out of their rice cooker and learn about the many dishes that can be made with this versatile kitchen appliance.

How to Use Your Zojirushi Cooker?

● ● ●

Utilizing your Zojirushi rice cooker is a simple process that can consistently produce excellent outcomes. Click on the links below to learn how to use your appliance properly:

You will read the manual carefully before using your Zojirushi rice cooker. Your model's specific features and functions will become more familiar to you after doing this.

Figure out how much rice you want using the measuring cup with the package. For exact measurements, check your user manual or look at the Zojirushi model you have. Make the Rice Runny: Run cold water over the rice until the water is clear. As a result, the rice will be fluffy when it's done.

Add Water: To calculate the right amount of water for the type and amount of rice you're cooking, use the water level markings inside the inner cooking pan. Usually, the numbers on the water level markers show how many cups of rice are supposed to be cooked.

Optional Additions: You can boost the flavor of the rice and water mixture by adding things like salt, butter, or herbs. Do not change the cooking process by going against the suggested ratios.

Insert the inner cooking pan: Put the inner cooking pan into the rice cooker and make sure it's securely in place.

Go to "Cooking Settings" and choose the right setting for your Zojirushi model and the type of rice you want to cook. Most Zojirushi rice cookers have settings for a variety of rice types, such as brown rice, white rice, sushi rice, and more.

You can start cooking by pressing the "Start" button after choosing the cooking setting you want to use. The rice cooker will switch between settings automatically to find the best cooking time and temperature.

Wait for Completion: Let the rice cooker end its cooking cycle. When the rice is done, most Zojirushi models automatically switch to "keep warm" mode. This keeps the rice warm until you're ready to eat.

Serving and Enjoying: Carefully open the rice cooker lid after the cooking cycle ends, and fluff the rice with a fork or paddle. Enjoy your favorite dishes with the freshly cooked rice.

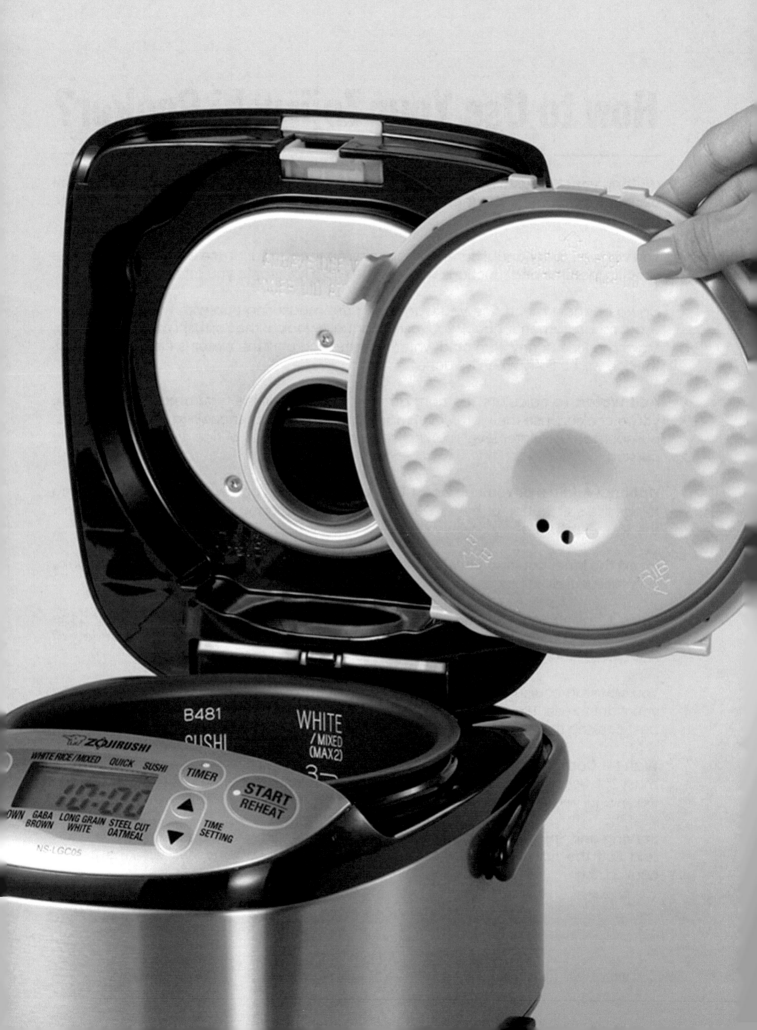

How to clean Zojirushi Rice Cooker?

● ● ●

It is important to clean your Zojirushi rice cooker to keep working well and last as long as possible. To clean your Zojirushi Rice Cooker, follow these steps:

Unplug the Rice Cooker: Make sure the rice cooker is not plugged in before you start cleaning. This will keep you safe from electrical hazards.
Wait to start cleaning the rice cooker until it's completely cool. If you don't, you could get burned.

Take Out the Inner Cooking Pan and Any Other Connectors: Remove any other connectors that can be taken out of the rice cooker and the inner cooking pan. Most of the time, these parts can go in the dishwasher, but check the instructions to be sure. Wash the outside of the rice cooker with a damp cloth or sponge. Using rough cleaners or harsh chemicals on the finish could damage it.

Clean the inner cooking pan: Use warm, soapy water and a soft sponge or cloth to clean the inner cooking pan well. Pay extra attention to any food that won't come off, and if you need to, use a soft brush. Use clean water to rinse the pan well.

Clean the Lid and Steam Vent: Wipe the lid and steam vent clean with a damp cloth to get rid of any food. Keep the lid out of water because it has electrical parts inside. Instead, clean it with a damp cloth.

Clean the heating plate: Use a damp cloth to wipe off any spills or stains on the heating plate at the bottom of the rice cooker. Scrubbing pads and cleaners that are rough can scratch the surface, so don't use them.

After cleaning, make sure to dry all the parts that can be taken off and the inside of the rice cooker well with a clean towel or by letting them dry naturally.

Assemble: Once everything is dry and clean, put the inner cooking pan back into the rice cooker and return any extra parts to the storage compartments where they belong.
Put the rice cooker away in a clean, dry place when not in use, and make sure the cord is wound up neatly so no one can trip over it.

If you do these things on a regular basis, your Zojirushi Rice Cooker will stay clean and in great shape for years of delicious cooking. It is important to read the user manual to find specific cleaning instructions and any maintenance tips the manufacturer gives.

1. SOFT & FLUFFY RICE COOKER BREAD

Prep Time: 15 Minutes | Cook Time: 30 Minutes

Total Time: 45 Minutes | Serving: 6

Ingredients

- ✓ 2 tsp vegan butter or margarine
- ✓ 160g bread flour
- ✓ 1/4 tsp salt
- ✓ 1/2 cup of + 1 tbsp lukewarm oat milk
- ✓ 1 tsp instant yeast (3g)
- ✓ 1 1/2 tbsp organic cane sugar
- ✓ 40g cake flour

Instructions

1. To a stand mix, add the sugar, yeast, oat milk, vegan butter, bread flour, and cake flour. For 30 seconds, knead at a low speed (setting #2). Then, for 5 minutes, knead at a medium-high speed (setting #4). When you use a bowl, do the same thing, but for 10 minutes, knead the dough with your hands.
2. Make a ball out of it and put it in the rice cooker. Set to 10 minutes to stay warm. After 30 minutes, or when the dough is 1.5 inches thick, turn off the "keep warm" setting and let it ferment some more.
3. Make a log of the dough by punching it down and kneading it a few times. Cut the dough into six equal pieces. Make small balls out of it again by kneading it. Put it in the rice cooker and set it to 10 minutes on "keep warm." Finally, turn off the "keep warm" setting. Let the dough proof for another 20 to 30 minutes, or until it grows to x1.5 size. Because each rice cooker is different, do a poke test to be sure. If you poke the dough, it should slowly spring back. It moves too quickly and needs more time. What if it doesn't spring back? It has been fermented too long. After the dough has been proofed, cook it in quick mode. When it's done, turn the bread over and cook it again on quick mode. The bread is ready when the second cycle is over.

2. RICE COOKER OATMEAL

Prep Time: 5 Minutes | Cook Time: 30 Minutes

Total Time: 35 Minutes | Serving: 2

Ingredients

- ✓ 1 tbsp agave nectar
- ✓ 2 cups of water
- ✓ 2 tbsp flaxseeds
- ✓ 1 cup of fruit finely chopped
- ✓ 1 cup of rolled oats not quick or instant oats
- ✓ 1/2 tsp cinnamon
- ✓ Pinch Himalayan sea salt

Instructions

1. Put everything into the rice cooker and mix it all together well.
2. If your rice cooker has more than one mode, set it to "Porridge," "Rice," or "Quick Cook." That's how long oatmeal should cook for. Press Start once you've chosen your mode.
3. Once the oatmeal is done cooking, taste it and add more agave or cinnamon if you think it needs it.

3. MILLET SWEET POTATO PORRIDGE

Prep Time: 10 Minutes | Cook Time: 1 Hour

Total Time: 1 Hour 10 Minutes | Serving: 4

Ingredients

- ✓ 4 cup of filtered water
- ✓ 1-2 sweet potato
- ✓ 1/4 cup of foxtail millets

Instructions

1. Get the millets clean.
2. Cut the sweet potatoes into little chunks after peeling them. About 2 1/2 cups of can be made from one large sweet potato or two small ones.
3. Put millets that have been washed into the inner pot of the rice cooker. Finally, put clean water into the rice cooker's inner pot. There should be 1 inch of water in the pot.
4. After that, put the sweet potatoes in the rice cooker's first pot.
5. To switch to the pre-set "porridge" setting, press the "menu" button. This setting takes one hour to cook. Press the "cooking" button to start cooking right away. To set the timer for later, like breakfast the next morning, press the "timer" button to switch between "timer 1" and "timer 2." Then, use the "▲" and "▁" buttons to change the end time, and finally press the "cooking" button to set the rice cooker to cook on the timer.
6. When the food is done, the rice cooker will play a ringtone and then go to the "keep warm" setting until it is turned off by hand.
7. To make the porridge more healthy, stir it with a laddle for one minute before serving. Press on the pieces of sweet potato just a little to help them mix into the porridge.

4. STEEL CUT OATS

Prep Time: 5 Minutes | Cook Time: 30 Minutes

Total Time: 35 Minutes | Serving: 2

Ingredients

- ✓ 3-4 tbsp brown sugar
- ✓ 1 cup of steel-cut oats
- ✓ 1 cup of half & half
- ✓ Water

Instructions

1. Prepare the Oats: One cup of steel-cut oats should be measured out using the measuring cup of that came with your rice cooker. Putting them in the rice cooker's inner cooking pan is suggested. Increase the amount of water until the "STEEL CUT OATMEAL" level is reached, or use 2 1/2 cups of as measured with a rice cup.
2. Start Cooking: Put the cooking pan inside the rice cooker. Plug the unit in, close the lid, and start cooking. If your rice cooker has it, choose the "STEEL CUT OATMEAL" setting. If not, choose the "PORRIDGE" setting.
3. Add Creaminess: When the cooking cycle is over, and the rice cooker says, "Keep Warm," take the lid off, stir the oatmeal well, and add the half-and-half and brown sugar.
4. Serve Hot: It's time to serve your oatmeal. It tastes best when you eat it warm.

5. RICE COOKER FRITTATA

Prep Time: 10 Minutes | Cook Time: 15 Minutes

Total Time: 25 Minutes | Serving: 2

Ingredients

- ✓ 1 cup of vegetables
- ✓ 1/2 cup of cheese
- ✓ 3-4 eggs
- ✓ Salt and pepper to taste
- ✓ Chopped or diced meat (optional)

Instructions

1. Spray cooking spray that doesn't stick inside the rice cooker.
2. Fry the eggs in a medium-sized bowl.
3. Add the vegetables (and meat, if you want) and mix them.
4. Use salt and pepper to suit your taste.
5. Put the whole thing into the rice cooker.
6. Cover the whole thing with cheese.
7. Press the "cook" button and put the lid back on the rice cooker.
8. For about 15 minutes, or until the eggs are set, cook the frittata.
9. Use a plastic spatula to carefully take the frittata out of the pan when it's done and place it on a plate. Serve it with toast and fruit after cutting it up.

6. SAUSAGE & GRITS BREAKFAST CASSEROLE

Prep Time: 10 Minutes | Cook Time: 1 Hour

Total Time: 1 Hour 10 Minutes | Serving: 6

Ingredients

- ✓ ½ cup of quick grits
- ✓ 2 cups of water
- ✓ 1 tbsp unsalted butter
- ✓ 2 eggs
- ✓ ½ pound breakfast sausage, cooked and crumbled
- ✓ ½ tsp salt
- ✓ ¼ cup of milk
- ✓ 1 cup of shredded cheddar cheese

Instructions

1. Mix the grits, water, and salt in the rice cooker's bowl. Click the "White Rice" setting after closing the lid. After about 30 minutes, when the rice cooker turns to the "Warm" setting, the grits are done.
2. Close the rice cooker and open the lid. Stir the grits and scrape the bottom of the pot. Put the butter and stir until it melts completely. Then add the cooked sausage and cheese while keeping the bowl in the rice cooker.
3. Mix the eggs and milk together in a different bowl. Add to the rice cooker's grits and mix in. Put the lid back on and press the "Quick Cook" button. The setting will change to "Warm" on its own in about 15 minutes. Fork out the rice, open the lid, and mix it around. One more time, cook on the "Quick Cook" setting with the lid closed. Turn off the rice cooker, open the lid, and serve right away when it automatically changes to "Warm" again.

7. RICE COOKER GRITS

Prep Time: 15 Minutes | Cook Time: 30 Minutes

Total Time: 45 Minutes | Serving: 2

Ingredients

- ✓ 1 tsp honey
- ✓ 2 tbsp butter
- ✓ 1/4 tsp salt
- ✓ 1/2 cup of corn meal
- ✓ 1 cup of water

Instructions

1. Put the corn meal, water, half of the butter, and salt in the rice cooker's inner pot. Mix well.
2. Different models have different ways to set the timer to "30 Minutes" or "Quick Cook." Either way, the grits need 30 minutes to fully cook.
3. If you want to stir the grits in the rice cooker after they are done cooking, carefully open the lid. Use a fork to break up any clumps and stir until the mixture is smooth.
4. Add more butter to the grits and sprinkle fresh honey (or cheese or any other topping of your choice) on top. Enjoy!

8. EDAMAME RICE

Prep Time: 15 Minutes | Cook Time: 30 Minutes

Total Time: 45 Minutes | Serving: 4

Ingredients

- ✓ ¼ cup of nametake
- ✓ ¼ cup of ochazuke wakame
- ✓ ¼ cup of shelled edamame, cooked
- ✓ 2 cups of rice

Instructions

1. Get the rice ready. The rice should be washed several times or until the water is almost clear.
2. Make the rice. (Use the same amount of water and cooking setting that you normally use for rice in the rice cooker.)
3. Add the ochazuke wakame to the rice when it's done cooking. Mix slowly with a rice paddle.
4. Add the name. Mix it again.
5. Put in the cooked edamame. Once more, mix until everything is well mixed.
6. All set to eat!

9. HONEY SOY CHICKEN & RICE

Prep Time: 15 Minutes | Cook Time: 35 Minutes

Total Time: 50 Minutes | Serving: 4

Ingredients

- ✓ 1 tsp cornflour
- ✓ 2 cups of chicken stock
- ✓ 2 Chinese lap cheong sausages
- ✓ 1 tbsp honey
- ✓ 2 tsp sesame oil
- ✓ ½ cup of Chinese Shaoxing cooking wine
- ✓ 2 tbsp soy sauce
- ✓ 2 cups of jasmine rice
- ✓ 600g chicken thigh fillets
- ✓ 4 dried shitake mushrooms
- ✓ 1 tsp dark sweet soy sauce
- ✓ 1 tbsp finely grated ginger
- ✓ 3 garlic cloves
- ✓ sliced spring onion (scallions), to serve

Instructions

1. For 15 minutes, soak the dried mushrooms in hot water to soften them. Take off the stems of the mushrooms and throw them away. Split the mushrooms in half.
2. Soy sauce, dark sweet soy sauce, sesame oil, and cornflour should all be mixed with the chicken.
3. Put the chicken, mushrooms, sausage, garlic, ginger, and rice in a large clay pot or heavy-based pot with a lid. A cast iron Dutch oven works great if you don't have a clay pot. Mix everything together well. Add the honey, Chinese wine, and chicken stock, and stir until everything is well-mixed. Cover it, set it on high heat, and slowly bring it to a boil. Cut down on the heat once it starts to simmer and cook slowly for 30 minutes or until the rice is soft and the liquid is gone.
4. Take off the lid. Sprinkle spring onions and a little sesame oil on top of the rice. Warm up and serve.

10. SAFFRON RICE

Prep Time: 5 Minutes | Cook Time: 20 Minutes

Total Time: 25 Minutes | Serving: 4-6

Ingredients

- ✓ 1/2 tsp dried crushed chili
- ✓ 2 cups of white jasmine rice
- ✓ 1/2 tsp saffron threads
- ✓ 1/4 tsp ground cumin
- ✓ 2 tbsp fish sauce
- ✓ 1 clove garlic, minced
- ✓ 1/2 tsp turmeric
- ✓ 2 1/2 cups of chicken stock
- ✓ Squeeze fresh lemon juice

Instructions

1. Place the pot over high heat and add the stock. Bring to a boil, then take it off the heat.
2. Add fish sauce (or salt), garlic, chili, cumin, saffron threads, and fish sauce to the hot stock. Mix well. Mix this together and add it to the rice cooker with the rice. Cover and stir.
3. Turn on the stove. When the rice is done, fluff it up with a fork or chopsticks. It's okay if the dried chili rose to the top; just mix it in.
4. Put the rice next to your main dish to go with it.

11. BASMATI RICE

Prep Time: 5 Minutes | Cook Time: 25 Minutes

Total Time: 30 Minutes | Serving: 4

Ingredients

- ✓ 1 cup of (185g) aged, long grain basmati rice, brown or white
- ✓ 3/4-1 tsp kosher salt, or to taste
- ✓ 1 tbsp oil, any kind
- ✓ 1 3/4 – 2 cups of water

Instructions

1. If you want, you can wash the rice gently until the water runs mostly clear to remove extra starch. To drain well, use a colander.
2. Put the salt, water, oil, and rice in the rice cooker and stir them all together.
3. Pick the Normal (Regular/Sushi) setting for the rice. Pick the Brown Rice Setting for brown rice.
4. When the rice is done cooking, use a rice spatula or paddle to fluff it up and take it out of the cooker quickly so that it doesn't get soggy at the bottom. Keep the rice covered after cooking so it doesn't dry out or lose water.

12. QUICK WHITE RICE

Prep Time: 5 Minutes | Cook Time: 10 Minutes

Total Time: 15 Minutes | Serving: 4 Cups

Ingredients

- ✓ 4 cups of water filled to Line 2 in the rice cooker
- ✓ 2 cups of white rice Using the measuring cup provided by your rice cooker.

Instructions

1. First, rinse and drain the rice. Then, put it in the inner pot of the rice cooker. Add water to the pot until the line between the water line and Line 2 is met (about 4 cups).
2. Close the lid tightly and set the rice cooker to the RICE function. Then, put the inner pot inside the cooker. It will take 10 minutes for the rice to cook.
3. If the rice cooker is turned off, it will automatically switch to "Keep Warm." Let the rice cool down in the pot. Then, fluff it up with a fork or spatula.

13. LAP CHEONG RICE

Prep Time: 5 Minutes | Cook Time: 20 Minutes

Total Time: 25 Minutes | Serving: 1

Ingredients

- ✓ water
- ✓ jasmine rice
- ✓ lap cheong (Chinese Sausage)

Instructions

1. To find out how much rice you want, use the cup with your rice cooker. Two cups of rice is enough for three people.
2. After adding the cups of water, fill the rice cooker up to the line that says how many cups of water there are. Another option is to use the "finger trick": first, level the rice out, then measure the height of the rice along your finger. Add enough water to make the rice the same height as your finger when you rest it on top of the rice.
3. It's a good bet that each person will get one link of Chinese sausage. Then, turn on the rice cooker. It can steam both the rice and the sausage at the same time. Put the sausage slices on top of the rice.

14. BROWN RICE

Prep Time: 5 Minutes | Cook Time: 45 Minutes

Total Time: 50 Minutes | Serving: 4

Ingredients

- ✓ 2 cups of water
- ✓ 1 cup of short or long grain brown rice

Instructions

1. The first thing you should do is rinse your raw rice under running water. Even though this step isn't required, it gets rid of any extra starch that has been stored. When you add too much starch to your rice, it sticks together.
2. You should put in 1 cup of rice and 2 cups of water.
3. If your rice cooker has more than one setting, choose the brown rice setting. Put the lid on top and press the button to use the rice cooker.
4. After the rice cooker tells you it's done, let it sit for 5 minutes so it can soak up all the water. Then, slowly take off the lid, being careful not to get any steam on you. To make your rice fluffy, use a fork or a rice paddle. Now you can eat your perfect brown rice!

15. RICE COOKER PASTA

Prep Time: 10 Minutes | Cook Time: 20 Minutes

Total Time: 30Minutes | Serving: 4

Ingredients

- ✓ 2 1/2 cups of water
- ✓ 26 ounces marinara sauce
- ✓ 1 pound pasta
- ✓ meatballs or sausage (optional)

Instructions

1. You can add raw meat or sausage, but first, you need to cook them in the rice cooker pan on the Cook or Quick Cook setting.
2. Add any spaghetti or linguine that you have broken up into halves to the pan with the rice and any meat that you have. You won't have to break up some kinds of pasta to fit them in the pot. Put in sauce and water.
3. It's time to cook the rice. Mix it up often. Make sure the pasta is done when it turns off to warm. If it's not done yet, add water, stir, and cook again.
4. If you want to be vegetarian, leave out the sausage, meatballs, and ground beef.

16. SPANISH RICE

Prep Time: 5 Minutes | Cook Time: 30 Minutes

Total Time: 35 Minutes | Serving: 5

Ingredients

- ½ tsp garlic powder
- 1 can diced tomatoes with juice
- 3 bouillon cubes or 3 tsp Better than Bouillon
- 1 tsp cumin or smoked cumin
- 3 ½ cups of water
- 2 cups of white rice
- 1 small onion diced
- 1 tsp salt
- 1-3 tbsp chili powder

Instructions

1. Put the rice in the bottom of the rice cooker. Next, add the water and diced tomatoes. For the spices to mix with the water, add the onion and spices and stir them around a bit on top.
2. Follow the manufacturer's directions when cooking.
3. Taste the rice to see if it needs more salt after it's done cooking.
4. It can be a side dish or put inside your favorite tacos and burritos.

17. CORN RICE

Prep Time: 10 Minutes | Cook Time: 15 Minutes

Total Time: 25 Minutes | Serving: 3-4

Ingredients

- 1 tsp salt
- 2 tbsp cooking sake
- 2 cups of short grain Japanese rice
- 2 tbsp butter
- 1 small can corn
- Ground black pepper

Instructions

1. While the water is still cold, swish the rice around until the water runs clear.
2. Put enough water to reach the 2 cup of mark for white rice in the rice cooker's inner pot. Then add the rice.
3. Mix in the corn, sake, and salt.
4. To use the machine, close the lid, select "Plain," and press "Start."
5. Put the butter in after opening the lid.
6. Sprinkle some ground black pepper over the rice, then mix it all together well and serve.

18. VEGETABLE BIRYANI

Prep Time: 10 Minutes | Cook Time: 30 Minutes

Total Time: 40 Minutes | Serving: 4

Ingredients

- ✓ 1 fistful of mint leaves
- ✓ 1/2 tsp of turmeric powder
- ✓ 1/2 tsp of cumin seeds
- ✓ 1 tbsp of ghee
- ✓ 1 tsp of coriander powder
- ✓ 2 large onions sliced
- ✓ 1 small bunch of coriander leaves cilantro
- ✓ 1 tsp of red chilli powder adjust to taste
- ✓ 1 cup of basmati or any long-grained rice
- ✓ 2 tsp of biryani masala
- ✓ 2 cups of mixed vegetables chopped
- ✓ 2-3 green chillies minced
- ✓ 1 tsp of ginger garlic paste
- ✓ 1/2 cup of curd optional
- ✓ A few cashew nuts or almonds optional

Instructions

1. After you wash the rice, put it in water to soak while you prepare the rest of the food.
2. In a large pan, heat the ghee and roast the nuts if you want to use them. After you drain the potatoes, add the sliced onions and roast them until they turn golden brown. You can set half of it aside and mix in the garlic honey. Soak until it smells good.
3. After that, add the salt, turmeric, coriander powder, cumin, green chilies, and chili powder. It will take about one minute of cooking to make the spices toasty.
4. Add the chopped vegetables on top and mix well. Then add the biryani masala and the chopped coriander and mint leaves.
5. Add about 2 cups of water, the curd, and the soaked rice to the pan of your rice cooker. How much you use will depend on the type of rice cooker you have. When the rice is done, open the lid right away and stir it around while it's still hot. Add the roasted nuts and onions that you saved. If you want, you can add more coriander leaves and lemon juice as a garnish.
6. Serve with chips or papad and a nice raita to cool you down.

19. RICE COOKER FARRO

Prep Time: 5 Minutes | Cook Time: 30 Minutes

Total Time: 35 Minutes | Serving: 2

Ingredients

- ✓ 1 cup of farro
- ✓ 2 Cups of water
- ✓ Pinch of salt (optional)

Instructions

1. How to Measure and Rinse Farro: To measure 1 cup of Farro, use the measuring cup that came with your rice cooker. To get rid of any extra starch, rinse the farro well in cold water until the water runs clear.
2. Fill the cooker with the Farro. Clean the Farro under running water and then put it in the inner cooking pan of the rice cooker.
3. Put Water: Fill the pan with cold water. It usually takes twice as much water to make farro as farro itself. That means you need to add 2 cups of water to 1 cup of farro. Use a little less water if you want a firmer texture.
4. Soak: You can soak the farro in water for 30 minutes before cooking it if you want it to be softer.
5. Get started Cooking: Make sure the inner pan is in the rice cooker the right way. Keep the lid closed tight. To start cooking, plug in the power cord and press the cooking switch. The cooking light will let you know that the food is ready to be cooked.
6. Cooking Time: The Farro should be cooked for about 30 minutes, but because it is a whole grain, like brown rice, you may need to check to see if it's done and change the cooking time if necessary. You can add a little more water and start a new cooking cycle if the farro is still not soft after the first one.
7. Resting: After the cooking cycle is over, leave the farro to sit for ten to fifteen minutes. That way, it will be easier to soak up any extra water and finish cooking.
8. Fluff and Serve: Using a rice paddle or fork, fluff the farro after the time to separate the grains. Now your farro is ready to be used as a base for other dishes or as a side dish.

20. COCONUT RICE

Prep Time: 5 Minutes | Cook Time: 20 Minutes

Total Time: 25 Minutes | Serving: 8

Ingredients

- ✓ 1 tsp granulated sugar
- ✓ 1 can coconut milk
- ✓ 1 ½ cups of water
- ✓ 1 tsp kosher salt
- ✓ 2 cups of Jasmine rice

Instructions

1. Use a fine mesh strainer or rice colander to run cold water over the jasmine rice until the water runs clear.
2. Make sure the rice is completely dry before putting it in the rice cooker. You can either tap it against the sink or press on it with a spoon.
3. Then, put everything into the insert of a big rice cooker. Put the lid on top and press the "cook" or "white rice" button.
4. Use a fork to fluff the rice when it's done, and serve!

21. RICE COOKER ORZO

Prep Time: 5 Minutes | Cook Time: 15 Minutes

Total Time: 20 Minutes | Serving: 3 Cup

Ingredients

- ✓ 1 cup of orzo pasta
- ✓ 2 cups of water
- ✓ 1 tsp olive oil
- ✓ Pinch of salt

Instructions

1. After putting everything into the rice cooker, you should turn it on. The orzo will soak up the water as it cooks.
2. The rice cooker should be turned off, and the pasta should be al dente. Then, use a fork to fluff the rice. Most of the time, it takes 15 to 20 minutes for a rice cooker to cook orzo.

22. CILANTRO LIME RICE

Prep Time: 10 Minutes | Cook Time: 20 Minutes

Total Time: 30 Minutes | Serving: 8

Ingredients

- ✓ 2 cups of long grain white rice
- ✓ 2 tbsp lime juice, freshly squeezed
- ✓ 1 lime, zested
- ✓ 1 tsp light olive oil
- ✓ 2 tbsp minced fresh cilantro
- ✓ 1 tsp kosher salt

Instructions

1. For 10 inches, heat the pan over medium to low heat. Add the rice and oil. Stir the rice and toast it for 5-8 minutes or until it turns golden and smells good.
2. Toast the rice and add salt to the rice cooker. Follow the manufacturer's instructions to fill the container to the right water level (for me, that's 2 inches), then put the lid on and start cooking.
3. Open the rice cooker and use a fork to fluff the rice when it's done. After that, put it in a bowl and add the lime juice, zest, and cilantro. You can taste it and add more cilantro, zest, or juice if you want.

23. VEGETABLE THAI CURRY

Prep Time: 15 Minutes | Cook Time: 40 Minutes

Total Time: 55 Minutes | Serving: 3-4

Ingredients

- ✓ 1 cup of snow peas
- ✓ 1 ½ cup of chopped broccoli
- ✓ 1 cup of coconut milk
- ✓ 1 small onion, chopped
- ✓ 3 tbsp Thai red or yellow curry paste
- ✓ 1 cup of water
- ✓ 1 tbsp brown sugar
- ✓ 1 red bell pepper
- ✓ 1 medium carrot
- ✓ 1 tbsp fish sauce

Instructions

1. Put the onion, carrot, bell pepper, snow peas, curry paste, water, and sugar in the inner pot of the rice cooker. Then, set the cooker to "Slow Cook." For forty minutes, set the timer.
2. Ten minutes into the cooking time, add the broccoli, coconut milk, and fish sauce.
3. Before serving, stir it up well.

24. MAC AND CHEESE

Prep Time: 5 Minutes | Cook Time: 15 Minutes

Total Time: 20 Minutes | Serving: 2

Ingredients

- ✓ 1 cup of uncooked macaroni noodles
- ✓ 2 ounce cream cheese
- ✓ 1/3 cup of milk
- ✓ 3 ounce medium cheddar, shredded
- ✓ 1 cup of vegetable broth

Instructions

1. Fill the rice cooker with water and put the macaroni and vegetable broth. Put the lid back on and set the cooker to "steam" for 5 minutes. It could take anywhere from 5 to 7 minutes to heat up before it starts counting down the 5 minutes of cook time. When the timer starts to run out, stir the pasta once. Then, when there are about two minutes left, stir it again. Every time you stir, close the lid right away.
2. Cut the cream cheese into pieces while the pasta is cooking. The pasta should have soaked up all the broth after 5 minutes. If not, cook for a few more minutes. Put the rice cooker on "keep warm" and add the cream cheese and milk. Mix the cream cheese in until it melts.
3. Last, add half of the shredded cheddar and stir it in until it melts. Do this again with the other half of the cheddar. If the cheese sauce gets too dry or thick, just put a little more milk and stir it in. Warm up and serve.

25. HERB LEMON RICE

Prep Time: 5 Minutes | Cook Time: 20 Minutes

Total Time: 25 Minutes | Serving: 4

Ingredients

- ✓ 1 tbsp coconut oil
- ✓ 1 tsp dried oregano
- ✓ 1 tsp dried basil
- ✓ 2 cups of stock
- ✓ ¼ tsp salt
- ✓ ½ lemon zested
- ✓ 1 cup of basmati rice rinsed

After Cooking:

- ✓ ½ lemon juiced

Instructions

1. Basmati rice, coconut oil, salt, lemon zest, dried basil, oregano, and stock should all be put into a rice cooker together. Use the "white rice" function to cook.
2. After cooking, add the lemon juice and serve.

26. SCALLOPS AND RICE

Prep Time: 20 Minutes | Cook Time: 1 Hour

Total Time: 1 Hour 20 Minutes | Serving: 4

Ingredients

- ✓ 2 cups of rice
- ✓ 1 tbsp sake
- ✓ ½ pound fresh scallops
- ✓ 2 tbsp butter
- ✓ 1 tbsp soy sauce
- ✓ 1.5 cups of water
- ✓ 2 tbsp chopped green onions or chives

Instructions

1. Get the scallops ready. Season both sides of the scallops with a little salt. Put on a plate and put it in the fridge for 15 minutes. You don't have to cover the plate.
2. Get the rice ready. A few times, until the water is almost clear, wash the rice. Add the water, soy sauce, and sake to the rice pot along with the rice. Wait 15 minutes.
3. Take the seafood out of the fridge. Dry the scallops off and put them on top of the rice. The water will cover them. Don't stir.
4. Use the same setting on the rice cooker that you normally use to cook rice. This time, use the scallop setting. Wait 5 minutes after cooking.
5. Take the pot out of the rice cooker. Place the butter in the pan and use a rice paddle to mix the rice, butter, and scallops together.
6. Add the chopped chives and mix them in. Serve right away. You can eat this scallop and rice dish by itself, or you can add it to a bigger meal as a "fancy rice" side dish.

27. TUNA TAKIKOMI RICE

Prep Time: 15 Minutes | Cook Time: 45 Minutes

Total Time: 1 Hour | Serving: 4

Ingredients

- ✓ 1 can solid Albacore tuna
- ✓ 2 tbsp hijiki optional
- ✓ 1 carrot
- ✓ 2 tbsp soy sauce 2 tbsp sake
- ✓ 3 dried shiitake
- ✓ 2 rice cooker cups of short-grain Japanese rice 1.5 regular cups
- ✓ 1/3 cup of frozen corn
- ✓ salt to taste

Instructions

1. Fill the bowl with rice. Put in 2 cups of rice. Drain the rice three to four times after each wash. Put the bowl back into the rice cooker. Put the dried shiitake mushrooms in a small bowl with about half a cup of water. Let them soak for a while. Put the hijiki in a second small bowl with half a cup of water. Let it soak for a while.

2. Peel the carrot and cut it into rounds while you wait. Cut the rounds into half or quarter pieces depending on how thick the carrot is. When the shiitake mushrooms look full, take them out of the water (don't throw away the water!) and cut them into small pieces. Cut off the hard stem part and throw it away. Pour water out of the hijiki and throw it away.

3. Mix the rice with the soy sauce, sake, and water in which the shiitake mushrooms were soaked. Put water up to the 2 cup of mark and stir. You can add salt now. How much you add will depend on the kind of tuna you use. You can also leave out the salt and add it after you've tried it! Put in the carrot, corn, hijiki, shiitake mushrooms, and tuna pieces that have been drained. Mix the ingredients together by giving it a quick stir.

4. Put the lid back on and press "start!" Use a rice paddle to combine the rice when it's done cooking, and then serve!

28. TURMERIC BASMATI RICE

Prep Time: 5 Minutes | Cook Time: 30 Minutes

Total Time: 35 Minutes | Serving: 4 Cups

Ingredients

- ✓ ¼ tsp kosher salt
- ✓ 1 ½ cups of chicken broth
- ✓ 1 tsp minced garlic
- ✓ 1 tbsp melted butter
- ✓ ¼ cup of minced yellow onion
- ✓ ½ tsp turmeric powder
- ✓ 1 bay leaf
- ✓ 1 cup of basmati rice

Instructions

1. Set the butter aside for 15 to 20 seconds to melt.
2. Use a mesh strainer to wash the rice. Be sure to shake it well to get rid of any extra water.
3. Put the salt, onion, garlic, turmeric, bay leaf, butter, and rice in a pot. Also, add the bay leaf.
4. Put the chicken stock and mix everything together.
5. Depending on what it does, tell the rice cooker to cook or start.
6. Use a fork to fluff the rice when it's done, and serve.

29. COCONUT RICE WITH LIME

Prep Time: 5 Minutes | Cook Time: 15 Minutes

Total Time: 20 Minutes | Serving: 6

Ingredients

- ✓ ½ tsp Sea Salt
- ✓ 1 cup of Water
- ✓ 1 Lime - juiced
- ✓ 1 cup of Coconut Milk
- ✓ 2 cups of Jasmine Rice

Instructions

1. In a strainer, wash the rice well under cold running water until the water runs clear.
2. Add the coconut milk, water, and sea salt to the rice cooker. Mix well.
3. Start the rice cooker and choose the right cooking setting for it. When the rice is done, the cooker will turn off by itself. For an idea of how long it cook, check the manual.
4. Leave the lid on the rice for 10 more minutes after it's done cooking. This helps the rice soak up all the water, which keeps it from getting mushy.
5. Use a fork to fluff up the rice, then put the lime juice and salt to taste. Serve after fluffing again.

30. CHICKEN RICE WITH VEGETABLES

Prep Time: 30 Minutes | Cook Time: 30 Minutes

Total Time: 1 Hour | Serving: 1

Ingredients

- ✓ 2 Chicken thighs bone-in small
- ✓ 1 1/2 cup of Rice uncooked, may mix with soaked whole grain rice varieties
- ✓ 2 cups of Choice of vegetable
- ✓ Salt to taste and other spices

Instructions

1. Put chicken thigh pieces in a bowl and season them with salt, herbs, and spices. Let them sit for 30 minutes. Rinse rice in water until all the dirt is gone.
2. Put raw rice in the cooker and add enough water to reach the 1 1/2 cup of mark.
3. Put pieces of chicken thigh on top of the rice and start cooking.
4. Clean the vegetables, rinse them, and cut them into small pieces.
5. When the rice is almost done bubbling and has soaked up most of the water, put the vegetables on top of it. Put the lid back on and keep cooking.
6. When the rice cooker turns to warm, use a fork or toothpick to check if the chicken thighs are done. From the pierce, there should only be clear liquid coming out.
7. Enjoy while still warm!

31. HEARTY RICE COOKER PASTA LENTILS

Prep Time: 5 Minutes | Cook Time: 20 Minutes

Total Time: 25 Minutes | Serving: 6

Ingredients

- ✓ 1 can cooked green lentils
- ✓ 1/2 cup of frozen vegetable mix
- ✓ 3 cloves of garlic
- ✓ 1/2 medium white onion
- ✓ 2 cups of vegetable broth
- ✓ 25 ounce oil-free marinara
- ✓ 2 cups of fusilli pasta
- ✓ Salt and pepper, to taste

Garnish with (optional):

- ✓ Fresh basil
- ✓ Cashew parmesan cheese

Instructions

1. Put everything into an 8 cup rice cooker pot and mix it well until everything is evenly mixed. Make sure the liquid is at least 1/4" above the pasta and lentils.
2. Set the timer to "white rice" and cover it. Cook for fifteen to twenty minutes, stirring every now and then.
3. Take off the lid and let the Spanish rice cool for 5 minutes. Then add salt and pepper to taste. Add some vegan parmesan and fresh basil on top and serve.

32. TOASTED COCONUT RICE

Prep Time: 10 Minutes | Cook Time: 20 Minutes

Total Time: 30 Minutes | Serving: 2

Ingredients

- ✓ 2 cups of jasmine rice
- ✓ ½ cup of water
- ✓ 2 tsp granulated sugar
- ✓ 1 cup of coconut milk
- ✓ 1 cup of sweetened flaked coconut
- ✓ pinch of salt

Instructions

1. Rinse the rice well until the water is clear. Put the rice in the rice cooker.
2. Salt, milk, sugar, and water should be added.
3. Follow the directions on the rice cooker.
4. Toast the coconut flakes. Melt some butter in a small pan. As you stir often until it turns golden brown, add the coconut. Put it in a bowl.
5. Take out the rice and rinse it until the water runs clear. Add to pot, then add the rest of the ingredients. Add more water until it just comes up above the rice if the liquid doesn't cover it. Bring up the temperature. After three to four minutes, turn down the heat and let it simmer for fifteen to eighteen minutes. Take it off the heat and use a fork to fluff it up.
6. When the rice is ready to be served, put toasted coconut flakes. Flakes will get soft if you add them too soon.

33. BLACK BEAN CHILI

Prep Time: 10 Minutes | Cook Time: 45 Minutes

Total Time: 1 Hour| Serving: 6

Ingredients

- ✓ 2 cloves crushed garlic
- ✓ 1 can black beans
- ✓ 1 large can or box of chopped tomatoes
- ✓ 2 carrots diced
- ✓ 2 cans black beans
- ✓ 1 cup of vegetable broth
- ✓ 1 can vegetarian refried black beans
- ✓ 1 tbsp olive oil
- ✓ 1 tbsp cumin
- ✓ 2 tbsp chili powder
- ✓ 1/2 onion diced
- ✓ pinch of salt
- ✓ shredded cheddar for serving
- ✓ chopped avocado for serving

Instructions

1. Make a big pot with olive oil and onions. Set it over medium-low heat. Cook the onions until they become clear. Put in the garlic and carrots. Cook until the carrots start to get soft. Put the rice in a rice cooker and put the broth, tomatoes, cumin, and chili powder. Set the rice cooker to the fast cook mode and press start. (You could also leave it on the default setting.) Put in the black beans after the quick cook cycle is over, or 20 minutes after if your cooker doesn't have a quick cook setting. Cook for another quick cook cycle, or keep cooking on the same cycle. After the second cycle, add the refried beans and mix them in. The refried beans will get warm if you leave your rice cooker on "warm" while you set the table. Put some cheddar cheese and avocado on top.

34. PASTA AND VEGGIES

Prep Time: 5 Minutes | Cook Time: 40 Minutes

Total Time: 45 Minutes | Serving: 6

Ingredients

- ✓ 16-20 ounce frozen mixed vegetables
- ✓ 1 cup of frozen cut leaf spinach
- ✓ 3 cups of water
- ✓ 16 ounce gluten-free pasta
- ✓ 48 ounce pasta sauce
- ✓ vegan Parmesan cheese to taste

Instructions

1. You can thaw frozen vegetables ahead of time or heat them on high for 4 to 6 minutes until they are no longer frozen. (Mix it at least once while it's in the microwave.)
2. Put pasta, water, thawed vegetables, and pasta sauce in the rice cooker. Stir to mix and serve.
3. Put the lid on the rice cooker and set it to the white rice setting.
4. After about 20 minutes, carefully open the rice cooker and stir the pasta in the middle of the cooking. Close the cooker and let the food cook.
5. After the pasta is done cooking, stir it to mix it up and then put it in bowls.
6. Add some vegan Parmesan cheese on top, and serve.

35. RICE COOKER JAMBALAYA

Prep Time: 10 Minutes | Cook Time: 30 Minutes

Total Time: 40 Minutes | Serving: 4

Ingredients
- ✓ 1 package Zatarain's Jambalaya Mix
- ✓ 1 package smoked or andouille sausage, cut into 1/4 inch pieces
- ✓ 2 and 1/2 cups of water
- ✓ 1 tbsp oil.

Instructions

1. Start with the Sausage: If your rice cooker has a saute function, heat 1 tbsp of oil. Add the sausage slices and cook them for 3-5 minutes, stirring occasionally, until they turn a nice brown color. This step is crucial for adding a rich flavor to your Jambalaya.

2. Alternative Sausage Cooking Method: Don't worry if your rice cooker doesn't have a saute setting. Just put the sausage in a pan and brown it over medium-low heat. Move the sausage to a plate and set it aside after it has browned. This way will make sure that your sausage is cooked just right for the jambalaya.

3. Prepare the Rice Cooker: Add two and a half cups of water to the bowl. If you cooked the sausage in a skillet, don't forget to add any fat that was left over to the rice cooker. These drips are flavorful and will make your dish taste better overall.

4. Adding the Jambalaya Mix: Now is the time to put the Zatarain's Jambalaya Mix into the steamer. Make sure the mix and water are well mixed by stirring them together. This step is very important for making sure that the flavors in your Jambalaya are spread out evenly.

5. Combine Sausage with the Mix: Put the sausage pieces that have already been browned back into the rice cooker. Add them to the mix and stir to spread them out evenly. Adding the sausage in this way is the key to ensuring every spoonful of your jambalaya tastes great.

6. Set the Rice Cooker: Setting your rice cooker to the standard setting and closing the lid. Depending on the type of rice cooker you have, it may take anywhere from 20 to 30 minutes to cook. Don't worry about the timing; trust your rice cooker.

7. Let the Jambalaya Rest: Let the Jambalaya sit in the rice cooker for about 5 minutes after the cooking cycle is over. The flavors can blend during this time, making the dish more cohesive and tasty.

8. Final Stir and Serve: After resting, stir the Jambalaya to make the rice fluffy and ensure all the ingredients are well mixed. Now your Jambalaya is ready to be served. The spicy sausage, fragrant spices, and perfectly cooked rice make it a delicious dish.

36. TOMATO RICE

Prep Time: 15 Minutes | Cook Time: 30 Minutes

Total Time: 45 Minutes | Serving: 4

Ingredients

- ✓ 1 large onion, thinly sliced
- ✓ 2 Tbsp unsalted butter
- ✓ 3 Tbsp double-concentrated tomato paste
- ✓ 2 medium tomatoes
- ✓ ½ tsp ground cinnamon
- ✓ ⅓ cup of coarsely chopped cilantro
- ✓ ½ tsp ground turmeric
- ✓ 3 garlic cloves, thinly sliced
- ✓ 2 cups of long-grain white rice
- ✓ 3 Tbsp vegetable oil
- ✓ Kosher salt, freshly ground black pepper
- ✓ Plain whole-milk yogurt (for serving)

Instructions

1. Saute Onions and Garlic: You can heat the vegetable oil in your rice cooker if it has a saute setting. After you add the onion, cook until it turns golden brown. Put in the garlic, season with salt and pepper, and cook until it gets soft. Don't use your rice cooker for this step. Instead, do it in a pan on the stove.
2. Add Tomato Paste and Tomatoes: Add the tomato paste to the pan or rice cooker and stir it in until it turns dark. Put in the chopped tomatoes and cook them until they get soft.
3. Combine with Rice and Spices: If you use a pan, move the tomatoes, onion, garlic, tomato paste, and tomato sauce to the rice cooker. Place the washed rice, cinnamon, and turmeric in a bowl. Mix everything together.
4. Cook the Rice: Put in two and a half cups of water. Put the lid back on, stir the rice, and set the cooker to the standard white rice setting.
5. Rest and Add Butter: Leave the rice to cool for ten minutes after it's done cooking. After that, add the butter and use a fork to fluff up the rice.
6. Serve: Throw some chopped herbs on the rice and serve it with yogurt.

37. FRIED RICE WITH EGG

Prep Time: 10 Minutes | Cook Time: 40 Minutes

Total Time: 50 Minutes | Serving: 4 Cups

Ingredients

- ✓ ¼ tsp sugar
- ✓ 2 cloves garlic
- ✓ ¾ cup of frozen vegetables
- ✓ 1 ¼ cup of chicken broth
- ✓ ¼ cup of onion
- ✓ 1 tsp fish sauce
- ✓ ½ tbsp butter
- ✓ 1 tsp soy sauce
- ✓ 1 cup of Jasmine rice
- ✓ 1 egg, lightly whisked
- ✓ ¾ cups of Chinese sausage
- ✓ green onions garnish

Instructions

1. Use a mesh strainer to wash the rice. Be sure to shake it well to get rid of any extra water.
2. Put in the butter, garlic, onion, fish sauce, soy sauce, and broth. Then swirl it around to mix it.
3. On top of the water, put the vegetables, sausage, and beaten egg.
4. Depending on what it does, tell the rice cooker to cook or start.
5. When it's done, use a fork to fluff it up and sprinkle green onion on top. Serve.

38. RICE COOKER CONGEE

Prep Time: 30 Minutes | Cook Time: 40 Minutes

Total Time: 1 Hour 20 Minutes | Serving: 4

Ingredients

- ✓ 8 cups of water
- ✓ 1 cup of jasmine rice
- ✓ 8 ounce chicken thigh
- ✓ 2 green onions
- ✓ 1 Tbsp ginger slices
- ✓ Salt and white pepper (to taste)

Instructions

1. Prep the Rice: In a bowl, wash the jasmine rice with water that is clear. You can use a blender to blend the rice for a while to make it smoother. Take it off the heat and let it sit for 30 minutes.
2. Make the Broth: Put 8 cups of water, chicken, green onions cut in half, and ginger slices into your Zojirushi. Put the lid on top and turn the heat to HIGH until it boils.
3. Add Rice: Take out any foam from the broth and then add the rice that has been drained. Could you bring it back to a boil and stir it? If you want a smoother texture, you could cook it on the slow cook setting for an extra 30 minutes.
4. Cook the Congee: Turn the heat down to SIMMER and cook for 30 minutes. Stir every so often. If the congee seems too thick, slowly add more water until it's the right consistency.
5. Final Touches: Take the chicken out and shred it. Salt and white pepper should be added along with an extra cup of water. Put the chicken shreds back in. Before you serve, put sliced ginger, sesame oil, and thinly sliced green onions on top.

39. TERIYAKI SHRIMP AND RICE

Prep Time: 10 Minutes | Cook Time: 30 Minutes

Total Time: 40 Minutes | Serving: 4

Ingredients

- 1 cup of frozen peas
- 2 cloves garlic
- 1.5 cups of uncooked jasmine rice
- 2 Tbsp brown sugar
- 1/2 pound raw medium shrimp
- 1 small onion
- 2 cups of water
- 1 tsp grated fresh ginger
- 1/4 cup of soy sauce

Instructions

1. If your shrimp is frozen, put it in a colander and run cool water over it for a few minutes to thaw.
2. Cut the onion into small pieces and put them in the bottom of the rice cooker with the frozen peas (I didn't thaw them first). Put in the raw rice, minced garlic, and grated ginger. Add these things together and mix them.
3. After adding the shrimp to the rice, add 2 cups of water. Turn on the "white rice" setting and close the lid. It will start to heat up, and once the food inside reaches the right temperature, the timer will start to run out (12 minutes for my model).
4. After the cooking cycle is over, put the lid back on and let the rice rest for another 5 to 10 minutes on the keep warm cycle. Mix the soy sauce and brown sugar while you wait.
5. Finally, take off the lid and pour the soy sauce mix over the rice cooker's meal. Mix the sauce into the rice slowly with a rice paddle. If you want, you can serve it hot with sriracha or sliced green onions.

40. RICE COOKER QUINOA

Prep Time: 5 Minutes | Cook Time: 30 Minutes

Total Time: 35 Minutes | Serving: 6

Ingredients

- 2 cups of water or broth
- 1 cup of quinoa
- 1/2 tsp salt (optional)

Instructions

1. Rinse the quinoa.
2. You can use broth or water to cook the quinoa. You could use water if you're still determining what you're going to do with it. If you know what you want to do in the future, broth can be a good way to spice things up. Put salt in the rice cooker and turn it on. That's how long it will take to cook most of them.
3. As soon as it's done cooking, could you give it a quick stir with a fork?
4. About 3 to 4 cups of quinoa will be made.

41. CURRIED RICE AND SPINACH

Prep Time: 15 Minutes | Cook Time: 1 Hour

Total Time: 1 Hour 15 Minutes | Serving: 5

Ingredients

- 1 t quality sea salt
- 2 Cups of Basmati rice
- 3 Cups of Water
- Jalapeno pepper, to taste
- 2 tbsp Curry Powder
- 5 cloves garlic, pressed
- 1 10 ounce package of frozen spinach
- 1 Can or 1.5 Cups of Garbanzo beans
- 1 Onion, medium, diced

Instructions

1. Put everything into the rice cooker. Set the timer for the meal you want to eat.
2. When the timer goes off, come back and fluff the rice. Let it sit for another 10 minutes or so.
3. Take a bite and serve!

42. BALSAMIC DIJON CHICKEN WITH FARRO & MUSHROOMS

Prep Time: 20 Minutes | Cook Time: 1 Hour

Total Time: 1 Hour 20 Minutes | Serving: 4

Ingredients

- 1/4 cup of minced fresh parsley
- 2 shallots, minced
- 1 1/2 cups of low-sodium vegetable broth
- 4 5 ounce boneless, skinless chicken breasts
- 1 tsp olive oil
- 8 ounce cremini mushrooms, quartered
- 1 cup of farro

Marinade:

- 1 tsp extra-virgin olive oil
- 1 tbsp Dijon mustard
- 1/3 cup of balsamic vinegar
- Pinch each sea salt and ground black pepper

Instructions

1. Make the marinade: Put all the marinade ingredients in a bowl or a plastic bag with a zipper top. When you add the chicken, make sure the breasts are completely covered in the marinade by turning them over. Make sure the bag or bowl is closed and put it in the fridge until you need it.
2. Choose the "regular" setting on your rice cooker. Put one tsp of oil in the bowl of the rice cooker. Add the shallots and stir to coat. Then close the pot or put the lid on top of it. Stirring every now and then for about 5 minutes, until the shallots have softened. Add the mushrooms and stir them around a few times during the next 8 minutes. Keep the lid on and cook until the mushrooms are soft and have lost some of their water. Put the farro and cook for 3 minutes, stirring every now and then while leaving the lid off.
3. Add the broth and stir. Put the chicken on top of the farro mixture, discarding any extra marinade. Put the lid on top or close the rice cooker and set it back to the "regular" setting. It might take an hour, but that depends on the rice cooker. When the chicken reaches 165°F on the inside, it's done.
4. Put 3/4 cup of the farro-mushroom mix on each plate and then place one chicken breast on top of each. Spread the parsley out evenly on top.

43. GINGER CHICKEN AND RICE

Prep Time: 15 Minutes | Cook Time: 45 Minutes

Total Time: 1 Hour | Serving: 4

Ingredients

- 3/4 cup of hot water
- One 2-inch piece of fresh ginger
- 3 packed cups of baby spinach
- 1 1/4 pounds skinless, boneless chicken thighs
- 1 large chicken bouillon cube
- 1 cup of unsweetened coconut milk
- 1 cup of jasmine rice
- Kosher salt

Instructions

1. Mix the bouillon cube with hot water in a small bowl. The rice, chicken, and ginger should all be put in a rice cooker together. Put the spinach on top. Add the bouillon broth and coconut milk to the cooker—season with a little salt. Start the stove. The food should be ready in forty minutes, when the stove shuts off by itself. Wait five minutes. Use a fork to fluff up the rice, then put it in bowls and serve.

44. CHICKEN CURRY

Prep Time: 15 Minutes | Cook Time: 30 Minutes

Total Time: 45 Minutes | Serving: 2

Ingredients

- ✓ 5 1/5 ounces chicken thighs
- ✓ 3/4 cup of water
- ✓ 1/3 box Japanese curry mix
- ✓ 1/2 cup of chopped onions
- ✓ 3-4 small potatoes
- ✓ cooked rice, to serve
- ✓ 2 tbsp cooking oil

Instructions

1. Start the rice cooker and heat the oil in a pot.
2. Put the chicken and cook it until it turns opaque after the onions get soft.
3. After you add the potatoes, cook for a few more minutes.
4. After you add the water, cook for 25 to 30 minutes, or until the potatoes and chicken are soft.
5. Mix in the Japanese curry mix until it's all mixed in. Put on top of hot rice.

45. CHICKEN AND SAUSAGE JAMBALAYA

Prep Time: 10 Minutes | Cook Time: 45 Minutes

Total Time: 55 Minutes | Serving: 6-8

Ingredients

- 1 red bell pepper, diced
- 1/4 cup of chopped fresh parsley
- 1 tsp Creole or Cajun seasoning
- 13.5 ounces andouille sausage, sliced
- 1 1/2 cups of white rice
- 3 cups of chicken broth
- 3 green onions, sliced
- 1/4 tsp pepper
- 2-3 cloves garlic, minced
- 1 small onion, diced
- 3 tbsp butter
- 2 cups of cooked shredded chicken

Instructions

1. Warm up the butter in a big pan over medium-high heat. Put the pepper and onion, and cook for 3 to 5 minutes, until the vegetables are soft. Put in the sausage and garlic, and cook until everything is nice and brown.
2. Put the broth and rice in the rice cooker. Along with the chicken, add the sausage and vegetables that have been sauteed. Add the seasoning and pepper, and make sure to mix it well.
3. Put the rice cooker on to cook. Put the green onions and parsley to the rice when it's done, and serve right away.

46. ONE POT OYAKODON

Prep Time: 15 Minutes | Cook Time: 45 Minutes | Total Time: 1 Hour | Serving: 2

Ingredients

Chicken Marinade:

- ✓ ½ small white onion sliced thinly
- ✓ .6 to .75 pound chicken thigh boneless and skinless
- ✓ 1 tbsp mirin add water if you can't have alcohol
- ✓ ½ tbsp dark soy sauce (for color)

- ✓ 1 tsp sugar
- ✓ 1 tbsp soy sauce
- ✓ ½ tbsp instant dashi powder
- ✓ ½ tbsp oil neutral oil like avocado
- ✓ ¼ tsp salt

Garnish:

- ✓ 2 eggs (with a pinch of salt) beaten to 70-80% mix
- ✓ seaweed sliced thinly

- ✓ 1-2 green onion sliced
- ✓ togarashi optional

Instructions

1. Soak 1 cup of short-grain rice in 2 cups of water for a while. It is best to soak short-grain rice in water first because it can be hard in the middle if you don't.
2. Cut ½ of a white onion into thin slices.
3. Add ¼ tsp of salt, ½ tbsp of instant dashi powder, 1 tbsp of mirin, 1 tsp of sugar, ½ small white onion, 1 tbsp of soy sauce, 1 tbsp of dark soy sauce, and ½ tbsp of oil to a bowl. Mix well. After mixing well, set it aside.
4. Run water over the chicken thighs until the water is clear. That way, your chicken won't taste like a game. Cut your chicken thigh into pieces that are 1 inch long. Put the chicken pieces into the sauce from Step 3.
5. Strain the rice or use the same bowl you used before to wash it until the water runs clear. To ensure you add the right amount of water in the next step, ensure you strain all the water. The water should just touch the rice's surface. The chicken and onions will add moisture to the rice, so we don't need too much water. We don't want the rice to be soggy.
6. Put the rice in a pot and add ½ cup of water. Then, add the chicken and onions that were marinated in step 5. Put the pot in the rice cooker and press the "cook" button. If you don't have a rice cooker, follow these other steps to cook the rice.
7. To get 70–80% of the egg white mixed in, beat the eggs. Let it sit at room temperature.
8. Before you add the eggs, quickly open the lid and pour them in after the rice is done cooking. Close the lid and wait for 2 to 8 minutes. For runny eggs, it will take 3 minutes, 5 minutes for over-easy, and 8 minutes for well done. Depending on your rice cooker, you may need to press the button again.
9. Add some sliced green onions to the rice to make it look nice. The chicken and egg sauce comes on top of the rice in oyakodon, so mixing them is unnecessary. Have fun!

47. RICE COOKER CHILI

Prep Time: 5 Minutes | Cook Time: 35 Minutes

Total Time: 40 Minutes | Serving: 3

Ingredients

- ✓ 1 tsp brown sugar
- ✓ 1/4 tsp garlic powder
- ✓ 1 15 ounce can diced tomatoes
- ✓ 1/2 6 ounce can tomato paste)
- ✓ 1/2 Tbsp chili powder
- ✓ 1/2 tsp cumin
- ✓ 1 Tbsp olive oil
- ✓ 3/4 cup of water
- ✓ 1/2 tsp onion powder
- ✓ 1 15 ounce can kidney beans
- ✓ 1/2 pound ground beef
- ✓ 1/2 tsp salt
- ✓ 1/8 tsp cayenne pepper
- ✓ freshly cracked pepper

Instructions

1. Put the ground beef and olive oil in the rice cooker. Choose the "white rice" or "cook" function, depending on what your cooker can do. Close the lid and cook the beef. Open it for a moment every couple of minutes to stir and break up the meat. Do this for about 5 minutes or until the beef is fully browned. Many rice cookers, like the one I used, will heat up once the lid is shut, so remember to do that every time you stir the rice.
2. If the beef you are using has a lot of fat, drain the extra fat after it has browned all the way through. In a rice cooker, add the ground beef and stir in the garlic powder, cayenne, onion powder, brown sugar, salt, chili powder, cumin, and pepper. Then, cover the rice cooker and cook for one minute more.
3. Add the kidney beans, tomato paste, water, and diced tomatoes (with their juices) to the rice cooker. Make sure the kidney beans are drained. Mix everything together by stirring it.
4. Once more, close the lid and make sure "cook" or "white rice" is chosen. Then, let the chili simmer for 30 minutes. Make sure the chili doesn't stick to the bottom by stirring it every so often. Start the cycle over if the 30 minutes are up and your cooker is still cooking.
5. After 30 minutes of simmering, taste the chili and add more seasoning if you like. Then, serve with your favorite chili toppings.

48. CHEESY BROCCOLI RICE

Prep Time: 5 Minutes | Cook Time: 25 Minutes

Total Time: 30 Minutes | Serving: 6

Ingredients

- ✓ 2 tbsp dried minced onions
- ✓ 1 tsp table salt
- ✓ 3 cups of fresh or frozen broccoli florets
- ✓ 2 Tbsp butter
- ✓ 4 cups of chicken broth
- ✓ 1 tbsp minced garlic
- ✓ ¾ cup of grated cheddar cheese
- ✓ 1-1/2 cups of arborio rice
- ✓ Salt and pepper to taste

Instructions

1. Mix the rice, butter, minced onions and, garlic, broth, salt, and black pepper in the rice cooker. Mix everything together.
2. Close the lid on the rice cooker and press the down button on the cook switch. It will take about 25 minutes for the rice to cook.
3. Put broccoli and half as much water as it will hold in a small saucepan while the rice is cooking.
4. Over medium-low heat, bring to a boil—strain and set aside.
5. Add the broccoli and cheese when the rice cooker turns to WARM.

49. RICE AND LENTILS

Prep Time: 5 Minutes | Cook Time: 30 Minutes

Total Time: 35 Minutes | Serving: 6

Ingredients

- ✓ 2 tbsp minced garlic
- ✓ water as needed
- ✓ 2 cups of white rice
- ✓ 1 cup of brown lentils
- ✓ ¼ cup of olive oil
- ✓ 2 tbsp chicken stock concentrate
- ✓ 1 cup of pearled barley

Instructions

1. In a rice cooker pot, rinse the rice, lentils, and barley well and mix them. Add the olive oil, garlic, and stock concentrate and stir them in.
2. Fill the rice cooker up to the 4 1/2-cup of mark with water. Pour it over the foods.
3. For about 30 minutes, or until the rice and lentils are soft, press "Start."

50. CLAY POT CHICKEN RICE

Prep Time: 15 Minutes | Cook Time: 45 Minutes

Total Time: 1 Hour | Serving: 4

Ingredients

- ✓ 1 inch ginger
- ✓ 4 tbsp oil
- ✓ 3 rehydrated dried shiitake mushrooms, thinly sliced
- ✓ 2 rice cooker cups of rice
- ✓ 1 tsp sugar
- ✓ 1 tsp salt
- ✓ 4 cloves garlic

- ✓ 450 gram boneless skinless chicken thigh/breast, cut into 1 inch cubes
- ✓ 1 tsp sesame oil
- ✓ 2 Chinese sausages
- ✓ 2 scallions
- ✓ 1/2 tsp ground white/black pepper
- ✓ enough water to cook rice according to your rice cooker

Marinating sauce:

- ✓ 2 inch ginger
- ✓ 1 tbsp dark soy sauce

- ✓ 1 tbsp oyster sauce
- ✓ 1 tbsp light soy sauce

Instructions

1. Set the chicken breast aside for 15 minutes while you marinate it in the sauce.
2. The garlic and ginger should be cooked in a pan or wok with oil for two to three minutes, or until they smell good. Add all of the marinating sauce, the shiitake mushrooms, the Chinese sausages, and the chicken cubes. Season with salt, sugar, and ground black and white pepper. The chicken is done when it's no longer pink.
3. Put the rice in the pan or wok and stir it around until it's well mixed. Keep in mind that the rice still needs to be cooked; it was just added to the pan or wok with the other ingredients. Put everything from the pan or wok into the pot of your rice cooker. Add the water that your rice cooker says you need to cook the rice, and then drizzle with sesame oil.
4. Follow the "cook rice" or "white rice" setting on a more advanced rice cooker until the "keep warm" setting is reached. After 15 minutes, remove the lid and put the thinly sliced scallions. Use a paddle to fluff up the rice, and serve right away.

51. HAINANESE CHICKEN RICE

Prep Time: 5 Minutes | Cook Time: 20 Minutes

Total Time: 25 Minutes | Serving: 4

Ingredients

- ✓ 3 cloves garlic chopped
- ✓ 2 Tbsp sesame oil
- ✓ 6 chicken drumsticks approx 1 1/2 pounds
- ✓ 3 cups of chicken stock
- ✓ 1/2 inch of ginger cut into thin strips
- ✓ 2 cups of rice
- ✓ 1 dash ground black pepper
- ✓ 3 pandan leaves tied into a knot (optional)
- ✓ scallions for garnish
- ✓ hot sauce

Instructions

1. Put sesame oil on the drumsticks of chicken. Add a little black pepper on top. For about 20 minutes, let it sit.
2. Clean the rice and let it drain. Do this in a rice cooker.
3. Put in chicken stock, ginger, garlic, and pandan leaves. To fill your rice cooker with chicken stock, fill it up to the 2-cup of mark.
4. Put the drumsticks of chicken on top of the rice.
5. Press "Start" and wait for the rice to cook.
6. To finish the cooking process, take off the lid and let it sit for another 10 minutes.
7. Take the chicken out of the pan with the rice.
8. Use a fork or chopsticks to fluff up the rice.
9. Put chicken and hot sauce on rice.
10. Add scallions as a garnish.

52. RIBS AND RICE

Prep Time: 1 Hour | Cook Time: 35 Minutes

Total Time: 1 Hour 35 Minutes | Serving: 4

Ingredients

To Marinate The Ribs:

- ✓ 1/4 tsp white pepper
- ✓ 1 pound pork ribs
- ✓ 1/4 tsp dark soy sauce
- ✓ 1/3 tsp salt

You'll Also Need:

- ✓ 1/2 cup of carrots
- ✓ 2 cups of uncooked rice
- ✓ 3 slices ginger
- ✓ Water
- ✓ 2 tbsp oil
- ✓ 2 tsp light soy sauce
- ✓ 1 tsp salt
- ✓ 1/2 cup of water
- ✓ 1/2 tsp sugar
- ✓ 8 dried shiitake mushrooms
- ✓ 1/4 cup of peas
- ✓ 3-5 cloves garlic

Instructions

1. Pour the marinade over the ribs and leave them alone for an hour.
2. Set a wok over medium heat and put 1 tbsp of oil. Stir-fry the mushrooms until they turn caramelized. Take it out of the wok and set it aside.
3. Put one more tbsp of oil to the wok to cook the ribs and set it over high heat. Lower the heat to medium and put the sugar, ginger, and garlic after the meat has browned. After one minute, add the carrots, light soy sauce, and ½ cup of water and stir-fry again. Bring to a low boil, then cook for 5 to 10 minutes, or until almost all of the liquid is gone.
4. While the ribs are cooking, put the rice in the rice cooker and add the right amount of water for the type of rice you're using and the directions that came with the rice cooker. Now is the time to strain the mushrooms and add some of the liquid they were soaking in if you want to. You could also use vegetable, chicken, or pork stock instead.
5. Put the shiitake mushrooms and 1 tsp of salt and mix them in. Move the pot around a bit to make sure the rice and liquid are spread out evenly. Place the rib mix on top of the rice. Just put it in the rice cooker and press the button to start cooking. Your dinner is about to start.
6. These days, most rice cookers will tell you how long the cooking process is still going on. When you have 5 minutes left on the timer, open the rice cooker lid and quickly sprinkle the peas on top. Close the lid right away and let it finish cooking. Serve it when it's done!

53. BLACK-EYE PEA JAMBALAYA

Prep Time: 15 Minutes | Cook Time: 35 Minutes

Total Time: 50 Minutes | Serving: 8

Ingredients

- ✓ 1 1/2 cup of raw rice
- ✓ 1 pound smoked sausage sliced and browned
- ✓ 1 15 ounce can black-eyed peas with jalapeno
- ✓ 1 small bell pepper, chopped
- ✓ Creole or Cajun Seasoning to taste
- ✓ 3/4 stick butter
- ✓ 1 small onion, chopped
- ✓ 1 14 ounce can beef broth

Instructions

1. Cut the sausage into small pieces that you can easily chew, and brown them in a medium-sized pan. In a microwave, melt margarine.
2. Put everything into a rice cooker, mix it all together, and then press the button to cook it. It tastes great with coleslaw.
3. Let the rice cooker sit for 10 minutes after the bell rings.

54. TACO SOUP

Prep Time: 15 Minutes | Cook Time: 1 Hour

Total Time: 1 Hour 15 Minutes | Serving: 6

Ingredients

- ✓ 1 pound chicken breast
- ✓ 1/2 medium onion
- ✓ 1/2 cup of brown rice, raw
- ✓ 5 cup of chicken broth, low-sodium
- ✓ 2 medium carrot
- ✓ 1 cup of corn, canned
- ✓ 1 clove garlic
- ✓ 1 tbsp olive oil
- ✓ 1/2 cup of black beans, canned
- ✓ 14 1/2 ounce diced tomatoes, canned

Instructions

1. Cut up an onion and garlic and put them in the bottom of a HOT rice cooker with some oil. This will help them brown.
2. Cut up your chicken while the onions and garlic heat up in the rice cooker.
3. Put the chicken in the rice cooker and cook it until it turns brown.
4. Pour in chicken broth, tomato chunks, brown rice, and corn that has been drained. Rinse and drain the black beans. Peel and cut the carrots into small pieces.
5. If your rice cooker has a "brown rice" setup, turn it on. Otherwise, leave it on for at least an hour and a half.

55. CHICKEN AND RICE SOUP

Prep Time: 15 Minutes | Cook Time: 2 Hour

Total Time: 2 Hour 15 Minutes | Serving: 8

Ingredients

- ✓ 3 celery stalks, chopped
- ✓ 2 tsp parsley
- ✓ 2 tbsp butter optional
- ✓ 3 carrots, chopped
- ✓ 1 bay leaf
- ✓ 1 tsp thyme
- ✓ 1/2 tsp rosemary
- ✓ 3 tsp salt
- ✓ 3 chicken breasts
- ✓ 1 small onion, chopped
- ✓ 9 cups of chicken broth
- ✓ 1/2 tsp sage
- ✓ 3 garlic cloves, minced
- ✓ 1 cup of parboiled rice
- ✓ pepper to taste

Instructions

1. Put everything in the rice cooker in the right order.
2. Set the heat to low and leave it alone for two hours.
3. Take the chicken out of the rice cooker a few minutes before you serve it and shred it or cut it into cubes.
4. After you add the chicken back to the rice cooker, cook it for another 5 to 10 minutes.
5. Get rid of the bay leaf and put the soup in bowls for each person.

56. BROCCOLI WILD SOUP

Prep Time: 20 Minutes | Cook Time: 2 Minutes

Total Time: 2 Hour 20 Minutes | Serving: 8

Ingredients

- ✓ 1 ½ tsp dried thyme leaves
- ✓ 1 tsp marjoram leaves
- ✓ ½ tsp garlic powder
- ✓ 1 tbsp olive oil
- ✓ 1 tsp salt
- ✓ ½ cup of long grain white rice uncooked
- ✓ 3 cups of half and half
- ✓ 4 cups of vegetable broth
- ✓ paprika for garnish
- ✓ 4 carrots sliced
- ✓ ½ cup of wild rice uncooked
- ✓ ½ cup of sliced almonds toasted
- ✓ ½ tsp pepper
- ✓ 1 large yellow onion chopped
- ✓ 2 cups of broccoli florets broken into small florets
- ✓ 1 cup of shredded sharp cheddar

Instructions

1. Put the oil in a pan with a heavy bottom and heat it over medium-high heat. When the oil is hot, put the onions and cook them for about 10 to 15 minutes, until they are soft and beginning to turn brown. After you add the carrot, cook for another 5 minutes or until the carrot is soft. Put cooked veggies in the bowl of a 4-quart rice cooker.
2. Add the next eight ingredients to the rice cooker, starting with the broth and ending with the pepper. Stir to mix. Put the lid on top and set the heat to low. Cook for one hour, or until the rice is done and the vegetables are soft.
3. Cover and cook on low for an extra hour. Then add the half-and-half, broccoli, and shredded cheese. Add seasonings by taste.
4. Put the soup into bowls, top with paprika and almonds, and enjoy.

57. CREAMY CHICKEN WILD RICE SOUP

Prep Time: 15 Minutes | Cook Time: 2 Hour 5 Minutes

Total Time: 2 Hour 20 Minutes | Serving: 8-10

Ingredients

- ✓ 2 cups of water
- ✓ 2 bay leaves
- ✓ salt and pepper to taste
- ✓ 6 cups of low sodium chicken broth
- ✓ 3 tbsp butter
- ✓ 2 tbsp salt-free seasoning blend
- ✓ 3/4 cup of carrots
- ✓ 1/2 cup of all purpose flour
- ✓ 1 cup of onions
- ✓ 1 cup of uncooked wild rice blend
- ✓ 2 tbsp olive oil
- ✓ 2 cups of milk
- ✓ 4-5 cloves garlic
- ✓ 3/4 cup of celery
- ✓ 1 pound boneless, skinless chicken breast

Instructions

1. Run water over the rice to clean it. Onions, celery, carrots, garlic, bay leaves, chicken broth, water, and the seasoning mix should all be put into a rice cooker before the rice is cooked. On the high setting, cook for 1 hour and 30 minutes. On the low setting, cook for 7 to 8 hours. Take the chicken out of the rice cooker for the last half hour of cooking. Let it cool down a bit before using two forks to shred it.
2. After the rice is done, put the chicken that has been shredding back into the slow cooker. Butter and oil should be melted in a saucepan. After you add the flour, wait one minute and then serve. Slowly put the milk into the mixture while whisking it. Keep whisking until there are no more lumps. Let the mixture get creamier and thicker.
3. Put this smooth mix into the rice cooker. Use a stir to mix. In case it's too thick, you can add more milk or water to your liking. Add pepper and salt to taste.

58. DAIKON AND CHICKEN SOUP

Prep Time: 30 Minutes | Cook Time: 1 Hour

Total Time: 1 Hour 30 Minutes | Serving: 4

Ingredients

- ✓ 2 tsp salt
- ✓ 1 daikon, peeled and cut into sticks
- ✓ 3 cloves garlic, minced
- ✓ 2 inches ginger, peeled and bruised
- ✓ 1 tsp sugar
- ✓ 1 liter water
- ✓ 2 stalks scallion, thinly sliced
- ✓ ½ onion, finely chopped
- ✓ 2 stalks celery, thinly sliced, reserve the leaves for garnish
- ✓ 1 free range chicken (Indonesian: ayam kampung), cut into 4-8 pieces

Instructions

1. In a pot, boil the daikon for 10 minutes. Then, drain it and set it aside.
2. Warm up 2 tbsp of oil in a pot. Fry the garlic and onion for about 2 to 3 minutes, until they smell good. Place the chicken pieces and garlic in the pan. Cook until the chicken is no longer pink.
3. Bring the sugar, salt, and water to a boil. Turn down the heat and let it simmer for 30 minutes, or until the chicken is cooked and soft.
4. Put in the scallions, celery, and boiled daikon. Cook for another 3 to 5 minutes.
5. Put the mixture into bowls for serving and top with celery leaves.

59. BEEF STEW

Prep Time: 15 Minutes | Cook Time: 3 Hour

Total Time: 3 Hour 15 Minutes | Serving: 6

Ingredients

- ✓ 2 pounds beef chuck
- ✓ 1/2 pound cremini mushrooms
- ✓ 1 pound small red potatoes, halved
- ✓ 1 tsp smoked paprika
- ✓ 2 sprigs fresh rosemary
- ✓ 2 cups of low-sodium beef broth
- ✓ 3 sprigs fresh thyme
- ✓ 3 medium carrots
- ✓ 2 tbsp all-purpose flour
- ✓ 1 tsp granulated sugar
- ✓ 1 cup of red wine
- ✓ 3 shallots, quartered
- ✓ 2 tbsp tomato paste
- ✓ 2 tbsp olive oil
- ✓ Fresh parsley, chopped (for garnish)
- ✓ Kosher salt and freshly ground pepper (to taste)

Instructions

1. Preparation: Put the beef chunks, flour, smoked paprika, salt, and pepper in a large bowl. Mix everything together so that the flour and spices cover the beef all over.
2. Initial Cooking: Put the olive oil in the rice cooker and turn it on. Once it's warm, add the beef mixture, shallots cut in half, potatoes and mushrooms cut in half, carrot chunks about 1 inch long, thyme and rosemary sprigs. Put in the sugar, red wine, beef broth, and tomato paste after that. Mix all the ingredients together well by stirring them all together. Add a little more salt and pepper to the mixture, and mix it again well.
3. Slow Cook: Turn your rice cooker to the "Slow Cook" setting. To set the cooking time to 180 minutes, use the timer. Press the Start button to start cooking and make sure the lid is tight.
4. Taste Test: Carefully open the rice cooker after 180 minutes of cooking. To make sure the stew is just right, taste it. To make it taste better, add more salt and pepper and mix it in.
5. Serving: Using a ladle, put the stew into bowls for each person. Add a sprinkle of freshly chopped parsley to the top of each bowl to finish.

60. RED WINE STEW BEEF

Prep Time: 15 Minutes | Cook Time: 2 Hour 10 Minutes | Total Time: 2 Hour 25 Minutes | Serving: 3

Ingredients

- ✓ Celery 100g
- ✓ Tomato 200g
- ✓ Salt
- ✓ Butter 3 tbsp
- ✓ Thyme
- ✓ Onion
- ✓ Red wine
- ✓ Sugar
- ✓ Mushroom 150g
- ✓ Tomato Paste
- ✓ Flour
- ✓ Beef Brisket 500g
- ✓ Garlic
- ✓ Carrot 150g
- ✓ Potato 150g

Instructions

1. Make cubes out of the beef. With flour on it.
2. Put butter in a pan that is hot. Cook beef in a pan until it turns golden.
3. Take out the beef. Put in the garlic and onion. Make a stir-fry.
4. Put in the celery and tomato.
5. Put the stir-fried food into the Mini Smart Cooker.
6. Put in the beef, potato, carrot, tomato paste, and thyme.
7. Add red wine to the beef.
8. Pick "stew" and set the timer for two hours.
9. Just before the time is up, add the mushrooms.

61. HEARTY TOMATO SOUP

Prep Time: 5 Minutes | Cook Time: 40 Minutes | Total Time: 45 Minutes | Serving: 6

Ingredients

- ✓ 1 small onion, diced
- ✓ 1 tsp Italian seasoning
- ✓ 4 cups of broth or water
- ✓ 1 cup of red lentils
- ✓ 3 garlic cloves
- ✓ 28 ounce can diced tomatoes with juice
- ✓ Salt, black or red pepper to taste
- ✓ 1 Tbsp butter, optional

Instructions

1. Put everything except the butter in a rice cooker and stir it around.
2. Cook. It only has an on/off button on mine. It's not flashy.)
3. Add the butter.
4. Make the soup smooth by blending it with a blender or an immersion blender.
5. Serve right away and enjoy with regular grilled cheese or just crackers!
6. If you're going to freeze or reheat the soup, be ready to add more broth because it will thicken as it cools.

62. JAMAICAN RICE AND PEAS

Prep Time: 5 Minutes | Cook Time: 30 Minutes

Total Time: 35 Minutes | Serving: 6

Ingredients

- ✓ 1 tbsp yellow onion
- ✓ ¼ tsp scotch bonnet pepper
- ✓ 1 can red kidney beans
- ✓ 1 sprig fresh thyme
- ✓ ½ tsp dried thyme leaves (optional)
- ✓ ½ inch gingerroot crushed
- ✓ 2 stalks scallion/green onion
- ✓ 1 tsp salt
- ✓ 1 tsp onion powder
- ✓ ½ tsp black or white pepper
- ✓ 4 - 5 tbsp coconut milk powder
- ✓ ¼ tsp allspice powder
- ✓ 3 cups of white, parboiled or brown rice
- ✓ 1 tsp garlic powder
- ✓ 1 garlic clove crushed
- ✓ 6 - 8 pimento seeds
- ✓ 3 cups of water

Instructions

1. Add the rice to the rice cooker's pot after measuring it out.
2. Check the package of rice to see if it needs to be washed. If the rice has already been washed, don't wash it again.
3. Two or three times, wash the rice and then drain it all the way. Add the water to the pot of rice after measuring it. Before putting the canned peas in the pot, drain them.
4. Put in the coconut milk powder, all of the dried seasonings, and all of the fresh seasonings. Then, stir the pot.
5. Close the lid on the pot and put it inside the rice cooker. Just plug it in and press the "cook" button.
6. When the water starts to bubble, use the spoon that came with the pot to stir it, and then put it back together.
7. When the "cook" button lights up to let you know the rice is done, ensure it has the desired texture.
8. If the grains are too hard, add two tbsp of water and cover the pot with foil or parchment paper. Press the "cook" button again and put the rice cooker lid back on top of the foil or parchment. This will let the rice steam and "fluff up."
9. Put the cover back on and let the rice steam for 5 minutes more if the texture is right. If the rice is still a little wet, take the pot out of the rice cooker and press the "cook" button again. This will dry the rice out a bit.
10. Jamaican Rice and Peas are warm and tasty. You can eat it by itself or with Oxtail, Fried Chicken, Curry Goat, Baked Chicken, or vegetables.
11. Clean up and put any food that's left over in the fridge.

63. SPANISH CHICKPEAS AND RICE

Prep Time: 10 Minutes | Cook Time: 20 Minutes

Total Time: 30 Minutes | Serving: 4

Ingredients

- ✓ 1 cup of vegetable broth
- ✓ 1 Tbsp olive oil
- ✓ 1 15 ounce can chickpeas, drained
- ✓ 1 cup of long grain white rice
- ✓ 1 6 ounce jar quartered artichoke hearts, drained
- ✓ 1 15 ounce can petite diced tomatoes, with juices
- ✓ 1/4 tsp dried oregano
- ✓ 1 tsp smoked paprika
- ✓ 1/2 tsp ground cumin
- ✓ 1/4 bunch fresh parsley, chopped
- ✓ 1 fresh lemon
- ✓ 1/8 tsp cayenne pepper
- ✓ 1/4 tsp onion powder
- ✓ 1/4 tsp garlic powder
- ✓ freshly cracked black pepper

Instructions

1. In the bowl of the rice cooker, mix the rice, smoked paprika, cumin, oregano, cayenne pepper, onion powder, garlic powder, olive oil, and about 10 turns of a pepper mill to make fresh pepper. Fork the rice around until the oil and spices are mixed in.
2. Then add the vegetables broth, diced tomatoes (with juices), artichoke hearts (drained), and chickpeas that have been drained. Set the rice cooker to "cook" or "white rice" and put the lid back on top. Mix everything for a short time.
3. If you want the rice cooker to cook the mixture all the way through, set it to "keep warm" and leave it there for at least 5 minutes after the cook cycle is over. If you want to make sure everything is mixed, open the cooker and fluff and stir the mixture a few times.
4. Mix the chickpeas and rice together in a bowl. Put chopped parsley on top, and serve with lemon wedges. Put the lemon juice right before you eat.

64. CHINESE STICKY RICE

Prep Time: 1 Hour 15 Minutes | Cook Time: 45 Minutes

Total Time: 2 Hour | Serving: 4

Ingredients

Soak in water 1 hour prior to cooking:

- ¼ cup of dried shrimp
- 1 cup of sweet sticky rice
- ¼ cup of jasmine rice
- 3-4 dried shiitake mushrooms

One Pot Sticky Rice:

- ¾ cup of water
- 1 cup of sweet sticky rice
- 1 chinese sausage
- ¼ cup of dried shrimp
- ¼ cup of jasmine rice
- ¼ tsp salt
- ¼ tsp chicken bouillon optional
- 1 strip chinese cured pork belly
- 3-4 shiitake mushrooms chopped
- ½ tbsp neutral oil avocado

Garnish:

- cilantro optional
- sliced green onions
- knorr soy sauce or regular soy sauce to taste

Instructions

1. One hour before cooking: For a few hours, let the dried shrimp and shiitake mushrooms soak in room temperature water. Also, put water in sticky rice and jasmine rice and let them soak. Once the shrimp and mushrooms have been soaked, drain the water and rinse them twice or thrice. Put it away and get ready to chop the food.
2. If there is any pork skin on the belly, cut it off. After that, cut the sausage, pork belly, mushrooms, and dried shrimp into small pieces. Put away.
3. For sweet sticky rice and jasmine rice, wash it under running water a few times until the water is clear. To ensure you add the right amount of water in the next step, ensure you strain all the water. The water should touch the rice's surface. The meats will add moisture to the rice, so we don't need too much water. We want the rice to be smooth.
4. Put ½ cup of water into the rice. Then add the sausage, pork belly, mushrooms, and dried shrimp that have been cut up. Put the pot in the rice cooker and press the "cook" button after mixing the ingredients. That's right, the white rice setting on my Zojirushi rice cooker makes the meats and rice taste great.
5. When the rice is done, mix everything together and fluff it up. Add soy sauce, green onions, and cilantro (if you want), and serve. Put it in the rice cooker to keep it warm while you eat. Have fun!

65. MEXICAN RICE

Prep Time: 5 Minutes | Cook Time: 30 Minutes

Total Time: 35 Minutes | Serving: 8

Ingredients

- ✓ 3 garlic cloves minced
- ✓ 2 tbsp tomato paste
- ✓ 1 cup of cilantro chopped
- ✓ 1 tbsp chipotle paste
- ✓ ¼ tsp salt
- ✓ 1 red onion diced
- ✓ 1½ cups of long grain white rice
- ✓ 3 cups of vegetable broth
- ✓ 2 tbsp olive oil
- ✓ ½ tsp cumin
- ✓ 1 lime juice

Instructions

1. Wash the rice well in a sieve or colander. Set it aside after draining.
2. Put two tbsp of olive oil in a saute pan that won't stick and heat it over medium-high heat.
3. For two minutes, cook the red onion. Since the rice is already golden brown, add it and stir-fry for three minutes.
4. For another 30 seconds, add the cumin, tomato paste, chipotle paste, and garlic.
5. Put the vegetable broth and the Mexican rice you have already cooked. When you close the lid on your rice cooker, it will make white rice.
6. Let the rice rest for 10 minutes in a warm setting after the rice cooker has been turned on. Add the chopped cilantro to the rice after adding the juice of one lime.

66. SUSHI RICE

Prep Time: 5 Minutes | Cook Time: 30 Minutes

Total Time: 35 Minutes | Serving: 6

Ingredients

- ✓ 1.5 cups of sushi rice
- ✓ 1/4 cup of seasoned rice vinegar
- ✓ 2 cups of filtered water

Instructions

1. Put the rice and water in a rice cooker. Follow the cooker's "white rice" setting to cook the rice.
2. If you want to season the vinegar, do it all over the cooked grains when the rice is done. Be gentle as you toss everything around to spread the vinegar even more. If you mash the grains, they will get sticky.
3. It's now ready to be used for sushi.

67. GREEK LEMON RICE

Prep Time: 10 Minutes | Cook Time: 10 Minutes

Total Time: 20 Minutes | Serving: 8

Ingredients

- ✓ 1/2 medium onion sliced
- ✓ 1/2 tsp oregano
- ✓ 3 cups of basmati rice
- ✓ 5 cloves garlic sliced
- ✓ 1 large lemon - zested and then juiced
- ✓ 1 tbsp fresh dill - more for the top
- ✓ 1 tsp salt
- ✓ 1/2 tsp cumin
- ✓ 2 tbsp olive oil
- ✓ Chicken broth

Instructions

1. The water ran clear when I rinsed 3 cups of white basmati rice. I let the rice sit in the water while preparing the other things.
2. It heated up your olive oil in a saucepan over the stove. You can also add the cumin, oregano, salt, and onions. Make a sauce. Put in the lemon zest and three cups of drained basmati rice. Mix the lemon juice into the rice and make sure it is well covered with the olive oil, herbs, and lemon.
3. You can put it in the rice cooker or cook it on the stove.
4. The rice was very flavorful, so I put it in my rice cooker and added enough chicken broth to make it a little more than 3 cups.
5. Start it up! There you have it!
6. I added more lemon juice and fresh dill at the end. In some places, I read that you should add more butter at the end, but I didn't. It was tasty! I'm going to try adding butter another day because I never say no to butter.

68. CHINESE CHICKEN RICE

Prep Time: 15 Minutes | Cook Time: 45 Minutes

Total Time: 1 Hour | Serving: 2

Ingredients

Chicken Marinade:

- ✓ 1 tbsp soy sauce
- ✓ 1½ tbsp water
- ✓ 1 tbsp corn starch
- ✓ 1½ tbsp neutral oil
- ✓ 0.6 to 0.75 pound chicken thigh
- ✓ ½ tbsp shaoxing cooking wine

- ✓ 1 tsp salt
- ✓ 1 tbsp ginger sliced
- ✓ ½ tbsp 4 season spicy bake mix
- ✓ 1 tsp sugar
- ✓ 2 garlic sliced

Rice Cooker:

- ✓ 1½ cups of jasmine rice
- ✓ 1 sliced chinese sausage optional

- ✓ 1¼ cup of water
- ✓ marinated chicken

Garnish:

- ✓ 1 green onion sliced

- ✓ sweet soy sauce optional

Instructions

1. One-inch pieces of chicken thighs can be cut, or they can be left whole and cut after cooking. I cut up two garlic cloves and one tbsp of ginger.
2. To marinate the chicken, mix it with garlic, ginger, 1 tbsp of soy sauce, 1.5 tbsp of light olive oil, 1.5 tbsp of water, one tsp of salt, one tsp of sugar, ½ tbsp of spicy bake mix, 1 tbsp of corn starch, and ½ tbsp of Shaoxing cooking wine. Put it all aside after mixing it.
3. Five to seven times, until the water runs clear, wash 1.5 cups of jasmine rice. Getting rid of the starch in the rice helps it taste better. Ensure no water is left in the rice after you strain it. Now you know how much water you need.
4. After that, add ¼ cup of water to the rice. The water should touch the rice's surface. The chicken will add moisture to the rice, so we don't need too much water. We don't want the rice to be soggy.
5. (not required, but strongly suggested!) Put Chinese sausage slices on top of the rice.
6. Place the chicken that has been marinated on top of the rice. Do not add the liquid marinade to the rice, or it will become too soggy. Then, put the rice cooker on high. On the rice cooker, press the "cook" button.
7. After the rice is done cooking, leave it in the rice cooker for 15 minutes. It's tough, but this will help your rice be fluffier and more moist!
8. You can add green onions and sweet soy sauce to the rice as a garnish. Mix the rice and eat it while it's still warm to serve. Enjoy!

69. THAI MASAMAN CURRY

Prep Time: 20 Minutes | Cook Time: 2 Hour 30 Minutes

Total Time: 2 Hour 50 Minutes | Serving: 4-5

Ingredients

- ✓ 3 cups of cubed butter squash
- ✓ 4 ½ cups of low-sodium chicken stock
- ✓ 2 tbsp Masaman curry paste
- ✓ 1 tbsp Stevia brown sugar
- ✓ ½ cup of uncook brown jasmine rice
- ✓ 1 cup of chopped yellow onion
- ✓ ½ cup of lite coconut milk
- ✓ 2 tbsp fish sauce
- ✓ ½ cup of edamame beans
- ✓ ¼ cup of diced fresh ginger
- ✓ 2 chicken breast
- ✓ 2 cups of sliced carrots

Instructions

1. Gather the food and chop, cut, slice, or dice it.
2. Then, put them all in a rice cooker pot. Start with something that will take longer to cook, like chicken breast or butter squash, and then add the rest of the ingredients on top of that.
3. Put the chicken stock and light coconut milk into the rice cooker and turn it on. Use the brown rice button if your rice cooker has more than one button.
4. Allow two and a half hours of cooking. Put it in a bowl and eat it.

70. JAPANESE CHEESECAKE

Prep Time: 20 Minutes | Cook Time: 40 Minutes

Total Time: 1 Hour | Serving: 8

Ingredients

- ✓ 2 tbsp lemon juice
- ✓ 2 large eggs whites and yolks separated
- ✓ 227 grams cream cheese softened
- ✓ 40 grams cake flour approximately 5 tbsp
- ✓ 80 grams granulated sugar approximately 6 1/2 tbsp
- ✓ 200 ml skim milk I made it with skim milk
- ✓ powdered sugar for dusting on top of the cake

Instructions

1. Put the cream cheese in a big glass bowl. Your cream cheese must be very soft. If it is not, it will not mix well with the batter, and you will end up with little lumps of cream cheese. It can splatter, so cover the top of the bowl with a towel and heat it in the microwave for 10 seconds until you can whisk the cream cheese into a smooth frosting.
2. Add the egg yolks after the cream cheese has been whipped until it is smooth. Use a whisk to make the batter smooth. From my mistakes, I learned that mixing everything until it's smooth after adding a new ingredient is important. If you do, it will be easier to get rid of the lumps later. Mix in the sugar and mix the batter well with a whisk. Mix in the lemon juice with a whisk until the batter is smooth.
3. Mix cake flour into the mix. It's important to sort. The flour stays lumpy if you add it in. I even used an electric mixer to try to smooth out the lumps, but it didn't work. This is different if you sift it in; you only need to whisk it in a few times to make it smooth. While I'm not holding the sieve, I lightly tap it against my other hand to make sure all the flour is sifted through. I don't have a flour sifter, so this is how I do it. Sift in the flour and then whisk the batter until it is smooth.
4. Mix the milk into the batter slowly with a whisk until it is smooth.
5. Put egg whites in a clean bowl of a stand mixer. If you want the egg whites to whip properly, make sure that neither the egg whites nor the bowl have any oils on them. Use a high-speed mixer to whip the egg whites until stiff peaks form.
6. Three times, add the egg whites to the batter. Because you don't want to lose all the air that you whipped into the egg whites, add them slowly each time. It's okay if the egg

whites mix in only some of the way. After the egg whites are mixed into the batter, a few small lumps and streaks of egg white should still be left.

7. Grease the inside of your rice cooker pot very well. I used one because this recipe calls for 5 1/2 cups of rice. Add the batter to the pot. Close the rice cooker and press the "cake" button to turn it on. If your rice cooker doesn't have a cake setting, pick the white rice setting and press for a second cycle after the first one is done. Put the cake in the oven for forty minutes. Once the rice is almost done cooking, you can open the lid to check on the cake. There should be even cooking on the top of the cake, and it should bounce back when you touch it. The cake should also be pulled away from the sides of the rice cooker. How long it takes to cook depends on your rice cooker's size.

8. Carefully flip your rice cooker pot over by putting a plate on top of it. The plate should be able to hold the cake. Putting the cake in the fridge for at least an hour will help it set and bring out the full cheese flavor. If you eat the cake right away, it will taste eggy and not very sweet. It tastes different after it sets because it is sweeter, and you can taste the cheese. Before you serve, sprinkle with powdered sugar. Keep cake that has yet to be eaten in the fridge.

71. CARAMEL CAKE

Prep Time: 15 Minutes | Cook Time: 30 Minutes

Total Time: 45 Minutes | Serving: 4

Ingredients

- ✓ 5 squares of Caramel
- ✓ 50ml Milk (can use oat milk)
- ✓ 1 tsp Baking powder
- ✓ 2 Large eggs
- ✓ 100g All-purpose flour
- ✓ 50g Grapeseed oil
- ✓ 70g Cane sugar

Instructions

1. Prep the Flour: To begin, sift the all-purpose flour into a bowl to get rid of any lumps. Put the bowl away until you need it again.
2. Melt the Caramel: Put the milk and caramel squares in a bowl that can go in the microwave. Start by microwaving for 25 seconds. Take it out, stir it well, and then microwave it again for 10 seconds at a time. Break up the caramel into pieces and stir them into the milk between each burst.
3. Mix Eggs and Sugar: The big eggs and cane sugar should be mixed together in a different bowl. Keep beating the mixture until it turns a light yellow color, which means it's well combined.
4. Combine Dry and Wet Ingredients: Mix the flour through a sieve with the egg and sugar. Mix it up until it's thick and smooth. Add the caramel milk mixture and mix everything until it's well blended.
5. Cook in Rice Cooker: With care, pour the batter into the rice cooker's inner pot. Click the "Plain" setting on your rice cooker, close the lid tightly, and press the "Start" button. When cooking is up, take the cake out carefully and put it on a plate.

72. RICE PUDDING

Prep Time: 10 Minutes | Cook Time: 2 Hour 50 Minutes | Total Time: 3 Hour | Serving: 4

Ingredients

- ⅔ c rice long grain or short grain
- 4 c milk
- 1 tsp vanilla extract
- ⅓ c sugar

Instructions

1. Don't use the cup of that comes with the rice cooker. Instead, use a regular cup.
2. Mix the rice and milk together in the bowl of the rice cooker.
3. Put the lid back on and set the timer for six minutes.
4. Open the rice cooker and put the sugar and vanilla when the machine goes to the "Keep Warm" cycle. Stir the ingredients together until they are well mixed.
5. Put the lid back on and press "Reset" to start a second Porridge cycle. This should be done every 15 to 20 minutes until the consistency you want is reached. The rice mix will get thicker as it cools down. Just add more milk if it's too thick.
6. Serve hot or let it cool a bit and put it in the fridge for at least an hour.

73. MUFFIN CAKE

Prep Time: 15 Minutes | Cook Time: 30 Minutes | Total Time: 45 Minutes | Serving: 8

Ingredients

- ¼ cup of olive oil
- 1 ½ tsp vanilla extract
- 1 cup of skim milk
- ¼ tsp salt
- ½ cup of diced apple
- 1 ½ cups of bran flakes, crushed
- 1 cup of all-purpose flour
- 1 ½ tsp ground nutmeg
- 2 tsp baking powder
- 1 ½ tsp ground cinnamon
- cooking spray
- 1 tsp baking soda
- ½ cup of diced banana
- ⅓ cup of raisins
- 1 egg
- ⅓ cup of white sugar

Instructions

1. Use cooking spray on the bowl of the rice cooker.
2. In a bowl, sugar, mix the flour, baking powder, baking soda, and salt. Mix the bran flakes, milk, cinnamon, nutmeg, and vanilla extract in a separate large bowl. Let the bran flakes soak up a little of the milk for about 5 minutes. Put the egg and oil to the bran mixture and mix it all together. Stir the flour into the bran mixture until it is just combined.
3. Mix the apple, banana, and raisins into the batter slowly. Use a rice cooker that has been sprayed.
4. If you stick a toothpick in the middle and it comes out clean after 3 cycles, the cake is done. This should take about 30 minutes.

74. POACHED POMEGRANATE SPICED PEARS

Prep Time: 5 Minutes | Cook Time: 50 Minutes

Total Time: 55 Minutes | Serving: 4

Ingredients

- ✓ 2 cups of pomegranate juice
- ✓ 2 star anise
- ✓ 2 firm pears Anjou or Bosc
- ✓ 3 black cardamon pods
- ✓ 2 whole cloves
- ✓ 2 cups of apple cider
- ✓ One 1" piece fresh ginger peeled
- ✓ One 3" cinnamon stick
- ✓ Orange Cashew Cream for serving
- ✓ peel from one clementine

Instructions

1. Apple cider, clementine peel, cloves, star anise, cardamom pods, pomegranate juice, and ginger should all be put in the rice cooker. Put pear halves into the liquid for poaching.
2. Turn the rice cooker to "white rice" and close the lid. Cook for 50 minutes or until the rice is soft enough that a toothpick can easily go through it.
3. Take off the lid and flip the pears over. Wait an hour. After an hour, flip the pears over and let them sit again. You can also put these in the fridge overnight to strengthen the color and flavor.
4. Add Orange Cashew Cream on top.

75. CINNAMON APPLES

Prep Time: 20 Minutes | Cook Time: 55 Minutes

Total Time: 1 Hour 15 Minutes | Serving: 3-4

Ingredients

- ✓ 3 tbsp Cornstarch
- ✓ 2 tbsp Butter
- ✓ 1/2 cup of Brown sugar
- ✓ 6 Tart apples
- ✓ 1 tbsp cinnamon
- ✓ 1/8 tsp nutmeg
- ✓ 3 tbsp Honey
- ✓ 2 tbsp Chopped walnuts

Instructions

1. Use cooking spray on the inside pot of the rice cooker.
2. Put everything except the butter and chopped walnuts in a large bowl. Mix the ingredients together well until the apples are covered all over.
3. Put the mix in the inner pot of the rice cooker and cover it.
4. Pick the "Slow Cook" setting and set the timer for 45 minutes. Start by pressing "Start."
5. Open the rice cooker when it's done cooking and add the butter and walnuts. Leave it alone for 10 minutes with the lid on. It goes well with cookies or ice cream.

76. BANANA YOGURT BREAD

Prep Time: 10 Minutes | Cook Time: 40 Minutes

Total Time: 50 Minutes | Serving: 8

Ingredients

- ✓ 2 large eggs
- ✓ 1 tsp vanilla extract
- ✓ 1/4 cup of unsalted butter, softened
- ✓ 1 1/2 cups of very ripe bananas
- ✓ 1/3 cup of low-fat yogurt
- ✓ 1/2 cup of brown sugar
- ✓ 1/2 tsp baking powder
- ✓ 1/2 tsp baking soda
- ✓ 1/2 tsp salt
- ✓ 2 cups of flour
- ✓ 1/2 cup of white sugar
- ✓ 3/4 cup of walnuts, chopped (optional)

Instructions

1. Prep Dry Ingredients: The flour, baking salt, baking powder and soda should all be mixed together well. Never touch it again.
2. Mash Bananas: Get a fork or a potato masher and mash the bananas. Remember to put them away.
3. Cream Sugars and Butter: Mix the white and brown sugars with a hand blender or stand mixer when the butter is soft. One at a time, add the eggs and mix well after each one.
4. Add Wet Ingredients: Put the yogurt and vanilla extract and mix them in until they are well mixed in.
5. Combine All: Pour the dry ingredients through a sieve into the wet mix. Just enough to mix everything. The bread will be tough if you mix it too much.
6. Add Nuts: Add the walnuts and mix them in. You could also use chocolate chips, pecans, or shredded coconut instead.
7. Cook in Rice Cooker: Spread the stuff out in the pan for the rice cooker after you pour it in. Put the cooker on the 40-minute Cake setting and start cooking. Take the bread out of the pan and place it on a wire rack to cool.

77. BLUE VELVET CAKE

Prep Time: 15 Minutes | Cook Time: 1 Hour 30 Minutes

Total Time: 1 Hour 45 Minutes | Serving: 8 Slices

Ingredients

Blue Velvet Cake:

- ✓ 2 tsp royal blue food color
- ✓ 3 eggs
- ✓ 1 tbsp cocoa powder
- ✓ 1 box white cake mix
- ✓ ¼ cup of buttermilk
- ✓ ⅓ cup of oil

Cream Cheese Frosting:

- ✓ 8 ounce cream cheese
- ✓ 4 cups of powdered sugar
- ✓ 2 tsp vanilla
- ✓ ½ cup of butter

Topping:

- ✓ blueberry, optional
- ✓ chocolate shaving, optional

Instructions

1. In a mixing bowl, mix the blue velvet cake ingredients. Mix until it's smooth.
2. Put cake mix into the bowl of your rice cooker. Put the bowl in the rice cooker and set it to "slow." Wait 90 minutes.
3. Use a toothpick to see if your cake is done. If you put the toothpick in and then take it out and it comes out clean, the cake is done.
4. Take the cake out of the rice cooker after it's done cooking and let it cool for 15 minutes.
5. Turn it over, take it apart, and cut it in half. Put it in the fridge to make it easier to ice.
6. In a bowl, mix the frosting ingredients together. Mix until it's smooth.
7. Start with the cake's bottom half. Spread some frosting on it and, if you want, add some blueberries.
8. Put the other half of the cake on top. You can frost the cake in any way you like. If you want, you can add some chocolate shavings. Have fun!

78. RICE COOKER BROWNIES

Prep Time: 10 Minutes | Cook Time: 40 Minutes

Total Time: 50 Minutes | Serving: 4

Ingredients

- ✓ 50g Sugar
- ✓ 50g All-purpose flour or pancake flour
- ✓ 40g Pure cocoa powder
- ✓ 1 cup of Milk or unsweetened oat milk
- ✓ 5g Baking powder
- ✓ 1 Large egg, whisked
- ✓ Cooking spray

Instructions

1. Sift Dry Ingredients: The flour, cocoa powder, and baking powder should all be mixed together in a large bowl. That way, the batter won't have any lumps.
2. Add Sugar: Add the sugar to the things that have been sifted. Mix the dry ingredients together until the sugar is spread out evenly.
3. Mix Wet Ingredients: Crack a big egg into a different bowl and whisk it. Mix the egg that has been beaten with the milk of your choice. Mix the items together until the batter is smooth and free of lumps.
4. Prepare the Cooker: Lightly coat the inside of your rice cooker's pot with cooking spray. This keeps the brownies from sticking together.
5. Cook: Put the batter into the rice cooker pot that has been prepared. Pick the "Slow Cook" setting, close the lid, and set the timer for 40 minutes. Wait for the magic to happen after you press "Start."

79. CHOCOLATE CAKE

Prep Time: 15 Minutes | Cook Time: 1 Hour

Total Time: 1 Hour 15 Minutes | Serving: 8

Ingredients

- ✓ 1 tsp Baking Powder
- ✓ 1 and a half cups of Milk
- ✓ a dash of Salt
- ✓ 250 Grams Butter
- ✓ 1 tsp Vanilla Essence
- ✓ 3 large Eggs
- ✓ 1 and a half cups of Sugar
- ✓ 2 cups of All Purpose Flour
- ✓ 1 cup of Coco Powder

Instructions

1. Put all the dry ingredients in a large bowl and set them aside.
2. Get a big bowl and add the sugar to it.
3. Slowly melt the butter while stirring it all the time.
4. Mix the butter and sugar together with a whisk until the sugar is gone.
5. Whisk in the eggs until the mixture is light and fluffy.
6. Vanilla essence or vanilla sugar should be added.
7. Whistling the whole time, add all the dry ingredients.
8. Mix in the milk until it's smooth.
9. The rice cooker's sides and bottom should be greased. Put butter on it! It makes the cake taste better. Pour the mixture into the rice cooker. Just press "Start," and you're ready to go.

80. PANDAN CAKE

Prep Time: 20 Minutes | Cook Time: 50 Minutes

Total Time: 1 Hour 10 Minutes | Serving: 4

Ingredients

- ✓ 1 cup of Cake flour
- ✓ 1 ft long Pandan leaf
- ✓ 4 Eggs
- ✓ 3/5 cup of Sugar
- ✓ 3 1/3 tbsp Coconut milk
- ✓ Food coloring (green), as needed
- ✓ 2 1/3 tbsp Water
- ✓ Butter, as needed (for greasing the pot)

Instructions

1. Prepare Pandan Juice: Cut the pandan leaf into small pieces and mix them with water. Squeeze the fruit using a sieve or cloth to get the juice out.
2. Make Colored Coconut Milk: Add the pandan juice that has been squeezed to the coconut milk. For color, add a few drops of green food coloring.
3. Sift Flour: Sift the cake flour through a sieve into a bowl to ensure no lumps. This will make the batter smoother.
4. Prepare Egg Mixture: Take the whites and yolks apart. Whip egg whites in a clean bowl while slowly adding sugar until stiff peaks form. Mix well after adding the yolks one at a time.
5. Combine and Cook: With a spatula, add the sifted cake flour in three parts. Mix in the colored coconut milk two parts at a time until smooth. Put it in a rice cooker pot that has been greased. Tap it to remove any air bubbles, then set it to "Cake" and cook it for 50 minutes.

81. COCONUT RICE PUDDING

Prep Time: 10 Minutes | Cook Time: 30 Minutes

Total Time: 40 Minutes | Serving: 2

Ingredients

- ✓ 1/2 cup of water
- ✓ 2 tsp vanilla extract
- ✓ 3/4 cup of arborio rice
- ✓ 1 can coconut milk
- ✓ 1/2 cup of sugar
- ✓ a pinch of salt

Fruit Salsa:

- ✓ 10 strawberries, cubed
- ✓ Zest of 1 Lime
- ✓ 1 ripe mango, cubed

Instructions

1. In your rice cooker, put rice, coconut milk, water, salt, sugar, vanilla extract, and vanilla extract. If you want the rice to be fully cooked, cook it for 25 to 30 minutes after turning it on.
2. You can also put them in a heavy-bottomed saucepan over medium-low heat and cook them for the same time. Stir often to keep things from sticking.
3. At this point, the rice should be soft and cooked. Leave it alone and turn off the heat.

Fruit Salsa:

1. Step 1: Put the strawberries, mango, and lime zest in a bowl and mix them together. I like to let it sit for 15 minutes before putting it on top of my rice pudding. This lets the tastes mix for a while. Cover your tropical rice pudding with a topping while it's still hot and steamy. Then eat it right away. It's also good cold, but I like it better warm. Something about it makes me feel better.

82. BANANA CAKE

Prep Time: 30 Minutes | Cook Time: 1 Hour

Total Time: 1 Hour 30 Minutes | Serving: 8

Ingredients

Wet ingredients:

- ✓ 4 large size eggs, separate the whites from the yolks
- ✓ 100 gram sugar
- ✓ 100 gram unsalted butter, melted
- ✓ 2 ripe bananas, pureed with a food processor/blender
- ✓ 1 tsp vanilla extract

Dry ingredients:

- ✓ ⅛ tsp salt
- ✓ 1 tsp baking powder
- ✓ 1 cup of all-purpose flour, sifted

Instructions

2. If the inside of your rice cooker pot is Teflon, you don't need to grease and flour it. If not, please grease and flour the pot a little.
3. While adding the sugar in three parts, whisk the egg whites in a large bowl until they reach a medium peak.
4. Then, mix the egg whites with the banana puree, melted butter, and vanilla essence. You are mixing each ingredient all the way through before adding the next one.
5. As you use a spatula, slowly add the dry items (all-purpose flour, baking powder, and salt) to the wet ones. Be sure not to break up the airy batter by stopping before mixing the dry ingredients.
6. Put the rice cooker pot in the oven and pour the batter. Hit the "cook" button. Wait 10 minutes after it gets "warm." One more time, do the "cook" and "warm" cycle three more times, for a total of four times.
7. Take the lid off the rice cooker and use a cake tester to check if the cake is done. If the cake is still not done, follow the "cook" and "warm" steps again until it is done.
8. Turn the pot upside down, cover it with a plate that is wider than the opening in the pot, and take the pot out of the rice cooker. The banana cake should fall right onto the plate.
9. Serve the cake by cutting it into serving sizes.

83. UPSIDE DOWN PINEAPPLE CAKE

Prep Time: 30 Minutes | Cook Time: 1 Hour | Total Time: 1 Hour 30 Minutes | Serving: 8

Ingredients

Pineapple rings and juice:

- ✓ 1 to 2 pineapple
- ✓ 2 tbsp brown sugar
- ✓ 1 cinnamon stick
- ✓ 4 cloves

Wet ingredients:

- ✓ ¼ cup of sugar
- ✓ 50 gram butter, melted
- ✓ ¼ cup of milk
- ✓ 4 eggs, separate the whites from the yolks
- ✓ 1 tsp vanilla essence

Dry ingredients:

- ✓ ⅛ tsp salt
- ✓ 1 tsp baking powder
- ✓ 1 cup of all purpose flour, sifted

Instructions

1. Mix the brown sugar, cinnamon, cloves, and pineapple in a pan. Warm the sugar up slowly until it starts to bubble. When the pineapple is soft but still stiff, take it off the heat and let it soak up the juice while you continue to make the cake.
2. To make a medium peak, whisk the egg whites in a bowl. Add the sugar in small amounts at a time; I do this three times.
3. After that, mix the egg whites with the melted butter, milk, and vanilla extract. You are mixing each ingredient all the way through before adding the next one.
4. Finally, use a spatula to mix the dry ingredients with the wet ones. Only do this part a little, or all your work to get the air out of the egg whites will be for nothing. Just make sure that everything is well mixed.
5. Put the pineapple rings at the bottom of your rice cooker pot. Save the cooking liquid to use as a glaze on the cake. Cover the pineapples with the batter poured into the pot.
6. Put the pot inside the rice cooker and press the "cook" button. Wait 10 minutes after it gets "warm." Repeat the process three more times after the fourth "cook" and "warm" cycle.
7. Place a toothpick into the cake to see if it's done. If it comes out clean, the cake is done. It's done when the toothpick comes out clean. If not, continue the "cook" and "warm" cycles until the cake is done.
8. Cover the pot with a plate that is wider than the opening in the pot. Turn the pot over, and the cake should fall onto the plate.
9. Use the liquid you saved from cooking the pineapples to brush the cake's top lightly. If it makes it that long, this helps the cake stay moist even the next day. Add some powdered sugar, also known as confectioners or icing sugar.

84. RICE COOKER PANCAKES

Prep Time: 10 Minutes | Cook Time: 1 Hour 5 Minutes

Total Time: 1 Hour 15 Minutes | Serving: 8

Ingredients

- ✓ 1 1/2 cup 2% milk
- ✓ 2 1/2 tsp baking powder
- ✓ 2 eggs
- ✓ 1 tsp vanilla
- ✓ 2 cups of flour
- ✓ 1/4 tsp salt
- ✓ tbsp white sugar

Instructions

1. Combine the baking powder, flour, and salt together in a large bowl. Do a stir to mix.
2. Put the wet ingredients in a bowl and mix them together until they are well mixed.
3. While pouring, stir the wet ingredients into the dry ones. To make the batter smooth, mix it until there are no more lumps in it.
4. Cover the bottom and sides of the inner pot of the rice cooker with cooking spray. Try not to get the batter on the sides so that it doesn't catch fire as you pour it in.
5. Select "cake" on your fuzzy logic rice cooker.
6. There are 5 minutes of cooling time after opening the lid and starting the pancake.
7. Cut into cake-like slices and serve with any toppings you like.

85. TOFU CHIFFON CAKE

Prep Time: 20 Minutes | Cook Time: 40 Minutes

Total Time: 1 Hour | Serving: 3-4

Ingredients

- ✓ 2 tbsp sugar (or honey)
- ✓ 200g Pancake mix
- ✓ 100ml Milk
- ✓ 5 ½ ounces Silken tofu
- ✓ 2 Large eggs
- ✓ ½ tsp Pure vanilla essence

Instructions

1. Use cooking spray on the inside pot of the rice cooker.
2. Put the tofu in a bowl and quickly drain it. First, beat the tofu until it's smooth. Then, add the egg, milk, vanilla essence, and honey.
3. Mix the pancake mix in slowly with a whisk. When the batter is smooth, put it in the rice cooker's inner pot.
4. Put the lid back on and choose "Slow Cook." Turn on the timer and press "start." Put some whipped cream and fresh fruit on top.